YOUR REINCA

ALSO IN THE 'BRINGING SPIRIT TO LIFE' SERIES

A Child is Born, A Natural Guide to Pregnancy, Birth and Early Childhood
Wilhelm zur Linden

From Stress to Serenity, Gaining Strength in the Trials of Life
Angus Jenkinson

Homemaking as a Social Art, Creating a Home for Body, Soul and Spirit
Veronika van Duin

The Journey Continues . . . , Finding a New Relationship to Death
Gilbert Childs with Sylvia Childs

YOUR REINCARNATING CHILD

Welcoming a Soul to the World

Gilbert Childs and Sylvia Childs

Sophia Books

Sophia Books
Hillside House, The Square
Forest Row, RH18 5ES

www.rudolfsteinerpress.com

Published by Sophia Books 1995
An imprint of Rudolf Steiner Press
Reprinted 2005

A catalogue record for this book is available from the British Library

ISBN 1 85584 126 6

Cover by Andrew Morgan Design
Typeset by Imprint Publicity Service, Crawley Down, Sussex
Printed and bound in Great Britain by Cromwell Press Limited,
Trowbridge, Wilts.

Think how the whole conception of life changes if the gaze is widened from the immediate present the human individuality experiences through the different incarnations!

Rudolf Steiner
Reincarnation and Karma

Up to the change of teeth the child bears a very distinct character, shown in its wanting to be an imitative being; it wants to imitate everything it sees in its environment. From the seventh year to puberty we have to do with a child who wants to take on authority what it has to know, to feel and will. And only with puberty comes the longing in an individual to gain a relationship to the world through his or her own individual judgement.

Rudolf Steiner
Study of Man

The first part of a child's life, up to the change of teeth, is spent with the unconscious assumption: the world is moral. *The second period, from the change of teeth to adolescence, is spent with the unconscious assumption:* the world is beautiful. *And only with adolescence dawns the possibility of discovering:* the world is true.

Rudolf Steiner
Study of Man

Now the fact that people of the present day are particularly disinclined to believe in reincarnation and karma (self-created destiny) is connected in a remarkable way with their pursuits and studies—that is, in so far as these concern their intellectual faculties—and this fact will produce the opposite effect in the future. In the next incarnation these people, whether their pursuits are spiritual or material, will have a strong predisposition to gain an impression of their previous incarnation.

Rudolf Steiner
Reincarnation and Karma

Contents

Foreword

We were motivated to write this book as a result of our anguish and distress at the time when, a few years ago, the whole nation suffered in similar fashion when a toddler was brutally murdered by two young boys. Materially, of course, the boys stood trial, but the real shame, blame and responsibility should be placed squarely on the shoulders of society at large. Society did not condone this 'crime', but it certainly stands indicted for its coming about. It actively and eagerly seeks vicarious enjoyment in the violence, crime and other dehumanizing items provided and promoted in the name of *entertainment* by the strongly visual media of film, television and video, as well as by the printed word, and should therefore be arraigned on charges of compliance, if not aiding and abetting. Many people already know this, but powerful vested interests stand in the way of complaint, censure and condemnation. Society is bound by the silken ties of pleasure to the kind of entertainment the visual media declare to be 'compulsive viewing'. Most people know how insidious the wiles of television tycoons and their agents are, but do they complain? So the public gets the television programmes it deserves, and society pays the price.

Of course, we are not so naive as to believe that these factors are the primary cause of such a tragedy. The whole socialization process is responsible for it; and this assertion is incontestable. A child's entire environment, including not only the behaviours of family members and significant others on television as well as 'live', is imitated, for better or worse, from babyhood onwards. Furthermore, mainstream educational policies and practices ensure that children are pushed prematurely towards adulthood before childhood is truly experienced. One of the main purposes of this book is to demonstrate that *human beings are primarily of spiritual nature, and only secondarily of bodily nature.* Moreover, the attempt has been made to make it reasonably clear to general readers how these two natures complement each other in the process of maturation and development.

Each individual is free to accept or reject the reality of reincarnation, but even the most cynical reader, after reading this book, may reflect more deeply on the nature and destiny of every human being, and value each one more in terms of repeated earth lives. Comfort may be gained from this knowledge by all who suffer unimagined and apparently unendurable hardships that this is not the *only* life. Along with the principle of reincarnation must go that of self-created destiny, and these together are integral to the whole concept of personal, and indeed collective, *responsibility.* Thus, in very truth and deed, we may each be enabled to love our neighbour as ourself.

1. Welcome to Our World!

> *How like an Angel came I down!*
> *How bright are all things here!*
> *When first among his Works I did appear*
> *O how their Glory did me crown!*
> *The World resembled his ETERNITY,*
> *In which my Soul did walk;*
> *And ev'ry thing that I did see*
> *Did with me talk.*

Thomas Traherne
Wonder, St. 1

The miracle of birth

It is rarely the case that the birth of a baby is not a very happy and important occasion for those who have waited with eager expectancy for many months, or even years. It is still an event which evokes strong emotions of awe and wonder, joy and gratitude. In earlier times babies were regarded as a gift of God, or the gods, and it is not difficult to understand why. A 'new' human being confronts delighted parents as a 'finished product', complete in every way, and they have done little apart from providing the wherewithal for its conception. The wisest and cleverest of human beings could not produce something so wonderfully and perfectly made— *entirely out of their own resources.*

The astounding fact is that it is not the parents who produce their child; rather, the child is produced *through their agency* by powers that are far greater, cleverer and wiser than they. In his well-known book *The Prophet*, Kahlil Gibran puts this notion very clearly:

> And a woman who held a babe against her bosom said,
>   Speak to us of Children.
> And he said:
> Your children are not your children.
> They are the sons and daughters of Life's longing for
>   itself.
> They come through you but not from you,
> And though they are with you yet they belong not to
>   you.

Such thoughts are profoundly true, and every expectant mother and father should ponder them. They should take pause and wonder why it is that they, and the baby's grandparents, welcome 'the little stranger' with such rejoicing. But they are not welcoming a *stranger* at all! The child will, unless unfortunate circumstances attend the whole event, be their *nearest and dearest* in every sense. The love and mood of happy expectancy is rather because they are welcoming a well-loved visitor or relation whom they have not seen for a long time—*and this is more than likely the case*. It is virtually certain that destiny has brought the event about, and they should reflect on the likelihood of their having been sought out by the individuality who has arrived in their midst as if by magic. All they have had to do is make the 'invitation' plain, and powers and forces beyond their control saw to the rest. The thought is a very humbling one.

The prevailing mood is more often than not one of gratitude for the 'gift' of a child that is now 'theirs' (but only in the sense of Gibran's words quoted above), and of reverence towards the unseen powers which were involved in the process. Most people have respect for what are means and processes designed and effected by Mother Nature, and our ancestors were obliged to leave the mysteries involving conception and birth as such. To them it was something of a miracle, but a miracle they accepted and took for granted.

However, the mood of gratitude persisted, as did that of reverence for the very principle of life itself, as hinted in the Gibran quote.

The crown of creation

The human race has long been regarded as the crown of creation, with the rest of the natural kingdoms subject to it. From a certain point of view, we human beings can, with ample justification, be considered as containing all remaining three so-called kingdoms of nature within ourselves, these being subject to us and to serve our purposes. A biblical account of creation mentions the division of the material world into four kingdoms, namely, human, animal, plant and mineral, with the human kingdom supreme and dominant. It is of course true that we share the characteristics of all three lower kingdoms, and in ways which are not immediately apparent.

It is obvious that in our external visible human form we are composed of minerals, chemicals and other elements of *matter* that constitute our purely physical-material principle—our physical body. All these substances are of course taken from the earth beneath our feet in the form of the various foodstuffs we need to sustain life. The main characteristic of the mineral world is that it is life-*less*, whereas the plants that we eat (and perhaps the meat from animals that eat plant material) are manifestly 'alive'. The difference between the mineral and the plant kingdoms is of course the ability of plants to take in and modify earthly matter into life-sustaining foodstuffs for the higher kingdoms—the animal and human. This *life-principle,* which is the main characteristic of the plant kingdom, is impossible to perceive directly. However, its presence is easily detected in the ability on the part of all plants to grow, procreate their species and—sooner or later—to wither and die.

These qualities of growth and propagation obviously

obtain in both animal and human kingdoms, manifested outwardly by the possession of not only a physical / mineral body, but a 'life-body', which gives form to and organizes earthly substances as appropriate to family, genus and species. This life-principle is referred to as a kind of *élan vital* (vital force) by some, and by others as the 'etheric body'. By definition, by reason of its power to organize, sustain and regenerate diseased or damaged cells and tissues that constitute the physical body, any entity that can be justifiably categorized as an *organism* necessarily possesses an etheric body.

Plants, with their purely vegetative life, have no power of mobility, and have no 'waking' consciousness as we and the animals have. Indeed, it is the possession of sense organs, and a system of nerves supported by a brain, that is the main characteristic of both animals and humans, and by reason of these the means of maintaining varying degrees of *consciousness*. This faculty is also organized in terms of awareness, perception and sensibility into a kind of invisible and imperceptible 'body' which is with some justification called the *astral* or 'starry' body. Feelings in the sense of *emotions* are present as part of this general state of awareness, more so in the case of human beings and less so in the case of animals, in which the instinctive factor of fear plays an important role in self-preservation.

The main difference between these two more highly evolved kingdoms of nature is the possession of a strong ego-sense in human beings which is absent in wild creatures. Animal behaviour varies enormously from species to species, but remains constant wherever they may be found on the earth: all pigs, cats, lions and so on act alike irrespective of wherever they happen to live, and their life habits are largely determined by their habitat, as reflection will show. Human beings, on the other hand, possess that factor of *universality* which animals do not; and within this universality exists the power of *individuality*. Human beings possess *faces*, whereas animals have widely differing types of features, and each person is a unique individuality, whereas the 'herd instinct' is paramount in the animal kingdom. The human ego represents the co-ordinating and initiating principle in each one of us, which as a constant observer preserves the past by reason of memory, experiences the present and, by conscious, responsible action, helps to determine the future for ourselves and possibly others.

Thus the human being is seen to be fourfold in nature, comprising (i) our ego or sense of individual selfhood; (ii) our astral body as bearer of a whole range of emotions, desires, likes, dislikes and so on; (iii) our etheric body which as a 'formative-forces body' maintains and supports (iv) our purely physical-material body as serving as the instrument necessarily employed in the performance of all our deeds and actions on the physical plane.

Assistance from the spiritual worlds

In respect of our fourfold constitution, it is our humble physical body of matter, organized and maintained by our etheric body, and thus representing our *corporeal* nature, that is the furthest advanced, the most sophisticated, the most perfect. It is far easier to control, as it were, than is our astral body, our 'consciousness-body', with its surging emotions, fleeting thoughts, impulses, contradictions, paradoxes and so on. Our spiritual member, our ego, by comparison, is embryonic in terms of maturity, power and controlling influence. Were it not so, we should all be perfect, and have no need to be on the earth at all! We are so weak in *spiritual* terms that when we find ourselves becoming involved with our corporeal members during the actual incarnation process, we are unable to control them and operate them adequately. This incarnation is such a slow process that it takes as long as 20 or so years before all four members— physical body, etheric body, astral body and ego—become fully integrated. This accomplishment is traditionally known as 'coming of age' at 21 years, when upon reaching adulthood individuals were by tradition given 'the key of the door' to Life.

When the incarnating individuality emerges from the realms of the spirit during the conception process, it needs an enormous amount of help and support; it is not capable, with its own limited resources, of accomplishing the process of embodiment into the material vehicle supplied by its parents. In the spiritual world before birth it was guided and sustained by spiritual beings of superior status to our own, more particularly the Angels, Archangels and Archai.[1] The long-established tradition of our each having a Guardian Angel, who guides us on our spiritual path, is true and sound. It is closely involved in all matters to do with our karma or self-created destiny, and it is especially during the first three years of life that these powerful, exalted spiritual beings help in the bringing about of the tremendous achievements that take place during those three first years. These are, in particular, the functions of *walking, speaking* and *thinking.*

It is at about the age of three that children begin to use the personal pronoun 'I', and this is indicative of the first significant involvement of the ego in their development. Very few of us are able to remember events that occurred before this age for, as mentioned elsewhere, the ego is involved in all matters of *self-consciousness* and *memory.* This fact has not escaped the notice of physiologists and psychologists who, moreover, are not able to explain the amazing speed at which infants learn to grasp the highly complex rules governing grammar and syntax involved in speech. Similarly, the rapidity with which the sensori-motor skills involving co-ordination and bodily and limb control are achieved is accepted as fact, even though 'scientific' reasons do not present themselves. It is when the child's own ego takes charge, as it were, that the learning process slows down; and the reason for this is that the spiritual beings gradually withdraw their support as the infant becomes more and more in *self*-control.

What is of profound significance is that parents, relations and significant others gradually take over the work of these spiritual beings in guiding the incarnation process; and the realization of this fact should do much to sharpen feelings of responsibility in family and carers. When the term 'descend' is employed in connection with the incarnating ego, this is literally true only with regard to the fact that it 'enters' the embryo when it is about three weeks of age, and then 'organizes' the formative growth-processes in a downward progression; that is to say, from the head downwards, as mentioned elsewhere (p 63).

'Out of the everywhere into here!'

When reference is made to the spirit 'descending' from the spiritual worlds, this is true mainly in a figurative sense, bearing in mind that everything more exalted, worthy of respect, imitation or even adulation is 'higher' than our own. Similarly, we speak of our higher and lower natures, ideals, aspirations, and so on. In fact, the spiritual worlds exist in and around us all, being diffused into—in the sense of permeating and pervading—everything. They are of course imperceptible to the human senses of a physical-material nature, and we are normally unaware of their existence in anything but the most general of circumstances. Before, during and after birth, the incarnating human entity, itself spiritual in nature, character and constitution, can also be described as permeating and interpenetrating not only the mother and her material (bodily) and immaterial vehicles (astral body and etheric body) but everything in its immediate environment as well—also of a sensory and supersensory nature and constitution.

In a very real sense, therefore, the incarnating spirit-filled ego experiences everything in its environment as *within itself rather than outside itself*. Indeed, it feels its surroundings as somehow part of itself, an extension of itself. As mentioned elsewhere, it has little choice but to allow this whole environment to influence it and 'work' upon it—and this mainly by the *imitation process*. While in the spiritual worlds prior to its 'descent' it had little choice but to imitate its milieu; and this was eminently worthy of imitation, permeated through and through and constituting by necessity and definition a thoroughly *moral* environment.

The eternal spirit can never be *born*

All this being so, the ego *per se* cannot in any sense 'be born', or 'have a childhood', being, as frequently asserted elsewhere, *birthless, deathless—immortal*. The physical vehicle of the incarnating entity is *born* of its parents, but the spirit-filled ego is 'born' into the child—as embryo—at about three weeks of age, as mentioned earlier. Thereafter it is the task of the ego to 'familiarize' itself with its new, physical-material vehicle for use during its earthly sojourn. By the same token, by making use of its material (bodily) sense-organs, as it is obliged to do by sheer necessity, it is able then to explore its environment 'in the physical', so to speak, as it previously did 'in the spiritual'. At first, of course, it has little notion of what this is, but as we all know the process of *growing into the world* has already begun—a process that commences during the embryonic stage, continues through the foetal stage and beyond birth, taking 7, 14, 21, 28, 35, 42 years and even longer to accomplish. The truth of lifelong learning is only now becoming realized as the reality it is: that education as a healing force enables each ego to progress further in its evolution. As we explain elsewhere, such education must be that based upon a knowledge of the whole human being in its many aspects, such as that given by Rudolf Steiner.[2]

The incarnating ego experiences the embryonic and foetal stages, and the first weeks after its bodily vehicle's physical birth *subjectively rather than objectively*. As it gradually, day by day, grows into the world, it experiences it equally gradually, *objectively rather than subjectively* — the other way round. To the extent that the growing child-entity experiences the world as object, to the same extent has its ego succeeded in its task of becoming incarnated. As mentioned elsewhere, the first stage is completed by the age of nine or ten, to be followed by others as mentioned earlier. Rudolf Steiner asserted that the very young baby does not show much in the way of curiosity or interest in its surroundings *because it is already familiar with them.*[3] This urge to explore and experience its environment for itself grows only gradually—and this is why no child should be over-stimulated, no matter how 'bright' it is, how intelligent.

Parents, eager and anxious to see how 'forward' their child is, readily succumb to the pronouncements of experimental psychologists and the incitements of toy manufacturers, especially those who specialize in 'early learning' apparatus which is purported to educate. But this they do at the peril of their offspring's future health and well-being. By artificially accelerating the normal maturational process in their zeal to 'bring on' or 'teach' their child, they call upon the powers and forces of its astral and etheric organizations far too early, thereby weakening them. Of course they are there to be called upon—but at the appropriate stage of maturation, namely, those of thinking at the stage of shedding its milk teeth, and those of judgement and causality at puberty.[4]

But, you will say, young children are always ready and eager to learn, so isn't it the right thing to do? Young children are always eager and ready to please their parents and others older than themselves, because for the most part they love them and wish to please them. They always respond to *encouragement* from whatever source it comes, and it is a wise parent who does not over-stimulate an infant simply because of this. Remember that whatever engages the will, and that means the performance of an action or deed, is appropriate during these early years. It is only by imitation that a child learns in a healthy, stressless way. It is the great responsibility of parents to, as it were, stand guard over their children, to *protect* them from the world, and this fact is rarely fully realized. When the whole organism is thereby precipitately 'forced' by any kind of coercion to learn by excessively engaging the memory, the resulting damage reveals itself in bodily and mental disorders only later in life, perhaps even in old age. These procedures are not exactly easy to understand and certainly not easy to describe, but it is hoped that a reasonably correct impression has been given.

Were you a *wanted* child?

It is easy to presuppose that every child is *wanted*, and that its arrival is eagerly anticipated. However, the virtually cavalier attitude towards abortion now prevalent is tantamount to constituting a form of birth control. And if the foetus has been found to be suffering from some kind of 'defect', e.g. spina bifida or Down's syndrome, mothers are automatically invited to have the pregnancy terminated. Where scanning is undertaken it is possible to identify the gender of the developing foetus, and this questionable practice may result in the abortion of girls in certain cultures. However, being wanted or not is never without significance to the incarnating individuality; for this it will certainly know. It is always most unwise to attempt to 'double-guess' an individual's destiny, for its workings are intricate to the point of being impossible even to surmise until well after important life-events have occurred, and perhaps not even then. We can have complete and utter faith in everyone's Guardian Angel in all this, for many decisions will have been taken before birth with the benefit of higher consciousness. Earthly decisions are often taken with expediency in mind; heavenly decisions are invariably long-term and with ultimate good in view.

It may be the case that an individuality is not successful in choosing its biological parents. But as always karma, *as self-created destiny*, may be relied on to 'do its best in the circumstances'. Adoptive or foster parents may be chosen by the incarnating ego for particular reasons, which may not be immediately evident to those concerned. It may be that if for some reason a child is unable to be born to its choice of parents, the child will be born into a family which lives near to those 'ideal' parents who did not procreate the child but are able to be in contact with it, so that it will still receive from them what it requires in the way of love, support and significant life-experiences, for example. Similarly, such a child might be born into the family of a close relation—the possibilities are numerous. However tangled karmic threads may become, it is certain that, in the long run, they will surely be unravelled.

> *In the science of spirit we get to know what it is that is given to us when a child is born. Each child bears within itself not only what is revealed to our senses, but also a spirit-soul being that has united itself to the physical embryo. And we learn how this spirit-soul being develops, just as we learn in material science how the physical nucleus develops under the influence of heredity. We see how something enters into the human organism that is supersensible, of a spirit-soul nature that is independent of inherited characteristics.*[5]

> Rudolf Steiner
> *Education and the Science of Spirit*

2. Gateway to the World

Out of the deep, my child, out of the deep,
Where all that was to be, in all that was,
Whirled for a million aeons thro' the vast
Waste dawn of multitudinous eddying light —
Out of the deep, my child, out of the deep,
Thro' all this changing world of changeless law,
And every phase of ever heightening life,
And nine long months of ante-natal gloom,
Thou comest.

Alfred, Lord Tennyson
Birth, from *De Profundis*

Pregnancy as a creative deed

Part of the miracle of birth is the amazing fact that each one of us has suddenly 'appeared' on the Earth, born of certain parents, at a certain time and in a certain place. All these factors are of enormous significance for the present circumstances and future prospects of every baby that is born. Helpless that they are, all children are entirely dependent on the nature and character of their circumstances. All mothers, as the main means by which material bodies are provided for reincarnating spiritual beings, are agents of the Divine Creative Principle, and as such are privileged individuals who act as its earthly agents. Pregnancy is a time when the results of active co-operation between human beings and exalted spiritual beings are manifested before our very eyes.

During pregnancy a mother's health and well-being is most important, for her own sake and for that of her baby's health during gestation, at birth, through childhood,

adulthood and even into old age. During this most significant event in a woman's life, when she is 'expecting', what
is happening to mother and embryo has results which are
not able to be fully apprehended at the time. Conception
may seem to take place by chance or mere whim, but the
results of the union are evident to parents and others as and
when the child begins to disturb the equilibrium of those
around it. Deciding to 'have a family' may be regarded as
inevitable in the terms of fulfilment for one or both parents,
but the realities, both seen and unseen, of giving birth to a
child are far more complex than science is aware of. The
Scottish seer and writer George MacDonald was aware
of all this:

> Where did you come from, baby dear?
> 'Out of the everywhere into here.'
> Where did you get your eyes so blue?
> 'Out of the sky as I came through.'[1]

The conception, gestation and birth of children take place
in proper sequence. The processes themselves are usually
entirely 'natural', which is another way of saying that they
are being brought about by means and in ways that are
beyond human control. It is of course undeniable that interference with these events is confined to that of a remedial or
corrective character by physicians or surgeons as best they
can. It is only when things go wrong that they take action.
Every birth is undoubtedly a *miracle*, for medical scientists
can only *describe* the incredibly wise procedures that unfold
from conception to birth. They are powerless to create
anything; at best, all they can do is to co-operate with nature.

The mixed blessings of pregnancy

At the commencement of pregnancy many women experience varying and mixed emotions. Whatever else, it is not an
easy time, and nowadays the demands on expectant moth-

ers are considerable, having to cope with matters of ante-
natal care, visits to doctor or hospital for examinations and
scans, as well as routine procedures such as ordinary family
duties. They are in effect leading double lives, out of concern
for their unborn baby as well as themselves. Feelings of joy
and elation are matched by depression if they are being
unwell with a 'morning sickness' that may last all day long,
feeling out of sorts, tired beyond imagining, having aver-
sion to food, and perhaps suffering from weepiness,
giddiness and fainting fits until about half-way through the
pregnancy.

Dr Norbert Glas has given profound, even wonderful,
insights into pregnancy and early childhood,[2] and we will
share these as and when they add weight to our discussion.
He explains that the symptoms arising in early pregnancy
are actually of spiritual origins in as much as there arises a
slight physical conflict between the developing embryo and
its mother. An expectant mother up to the moment of
conception has lived as an individual, her own person, so to
speak, and now she has to make way for her child. A
conflicting situation now arises whereby the mother must
at the same time put herself first in order to protect the
developing foetus, and put herself second in that she may
not be able to continue with her own interests and obliga-
tions. During pregnancy, the soul and spirit of the expectant
mother are to a certain extent displaced from her physical
body as the child is descending from the spiritual world and
gradually shaping its earthly body. However, later she is
more than compensated for this by the knowledge that she
can become conscious of a spiritual dimension to her own
condition by 'listening to what speaks to her inwardly'.
During this time she can become wiser by experiencing
what is taking place, as it were, between heavenly and
earthly principles.

It may be at this point of discomfort and weariness
in her pregnancy that if she does not realize fully what is

happening she may have misgivings about the whole process of bringing a child into the world. These misgivings may
be exacerbated if there are extraneous reasons for having a
baby, such as trying to save a marriage that is in difficulties,
wanting to be 'fulfilled' as a person, or selfish motives of
various sorts. Ideally, an attitude of selfless devotion should
be cultivated, but this is all very well when an expectant
mother is still expected to cope with household chores,
perhaps other children, and even the need to supplement
the family income. Nowadays, she may even be the family
breadwinner, with all the stresses and strains associated
with this, not to mention demands on her strength and
energy. In addition, modern traffic conditions, the burden of
shopping, and the general bustle and noise are hardly
conducive of inner peace and calm—and all she is longing
for is to put her feet up.

Dr Glas emphasizes that the inner life of an expectant
mother is of great importance, and benefits are to be obtained by contemplation of Raphael's pictures of Mary and
Child, not for any narrow sectarian reasons but because
in a purely artistic sense 'they are the right food for the soul
of a mother-to-be. Healing strength flows from the colours
and gestures in these pictures.'[3] He warns that television,
radio and cinema should be avoided because these media
'disconnect the human being from his and her spiritual
origin'. He continues:

> No human being who is interested in an inner devel-
> opment should be exposed to the noise of the radio first
> thing in the morning. Whatever experience one can
> bring out of sleep, and it may be only the feeling of
> being refreshed, is simply destroyed by the radio. A
> pregnant woman least of all should allow herself to be
> exposed to such an influence. In the evening an expect-
> ant mother should surround her child with loving
> thoughts. She should have a feeling of selfless devotion,

and it is difficult to foster such a mood when scraps of impressions from a television programme or a film are still dancing before her eyes. Finally, there is no need to discuss the evil effects of falling asleep to the noise of the radio at night.[4]

Mothers in this day and age are not always treated with the respect and consideration they deserve, and this affects their feelings of self-worth. Every expectant mother needs all the support she can get, from the father of her baby, from friends and relations, and from the wider community. She is, not unnaturally, apprehensive about what is going on inside her, and what will happen when the time for giving birth arrives. Well-meaning advice there will be in plenty, but this is no substitute for experience. She needs to be treated with sensitivity, for she may be feeling somewhat 'fragile' or even overwrought because of circumstances that are not immediately apparent.

Don't forget Father!

An expectant father may feel somewhat neglected, even rejected, and left out of things when friends and family make a fuss of the expectant mother. He may feel helpless and inadequate, not knowing how most effectively to help before the baby arrives as well as afterwards. As she retreats into her inner contemplations and ponderings, and fearing that he has lost his lover, friend and helpmate upon whom he depends, he may even harbour a desire to flee and never return. He may feel trapped in a situation in which he has lost his freedom, and is now faced with worries about money, retaining his job and general future prospects, wondering about his adequacy as a father and, perhaps most of all (especially if the baby is the first), whether he will be or has already been displaced in everyone's affections. It is vital for the parents-to-be to maintain free communication, for misunderstandings all too easily arise that in turn may lead on to inner or outer conflicts, which simmer unconsciously at that time and beyond. A reassuring hug works wonders!

Ante-natal classes may be useful for both partners, as much for the sharing of knowledge and experience with other people in the same situation as for information about their baby's physical development and successive stages leading to the actual birth. Any emphasis on exercise might well be misplaced, for deliberate strengthening of the muscles by exercising and massage is a toughening process, which is just the opposite of what is being brought about by nature itself. The body of the mother-to-be should rather become softer, more pliant and flexible, in the interests of the growing foetus. On the other hand, too much emphasis on relaxation and breathing exercises may result in her body becoming more flexible than is desirable, so that the foetus, having too much space, does not 'experience the resistance it should have for its natural development'.[5]

Be conscious of what you choose to do

Exercise taken by an expectant mother in ordinary everyday life, such as walking and doing ordinary housework while taking care to avoid heavy lifting or strenuous activity, is sufficient and suitable for her during a normal course of pregnancy. She should never tax her strength by lifting heavy objects—children included—or stretching up for things beyond her reach. Her diet should be wholesome, and include plenty of fresh vegetables, milk, salads, fruit and wholemeal bread. *Nothing but the best is good enough* for both mother and her developing baby in the way of freshly prepared ingredients. Processed food of the 'junk' variety is not as nutritious as that freshly prepared with loving care, and highly seasoned food should be avoided, as should alcohol. It is well known that smoking is detrimental to the health and well-being of both mother and child. Even the effects—and side-effects—of prescribed drugs should be thoroughly discussed with medical advisors, and however innocuous they may seem those freely available over the pharmacy counter should not be taken without the exercise of extreme caution. So-called illegal drugs must of course be shunned entirely.

Where will your baby be born?

The decision as to where the baby is to be born and who is to be present is usually made in consultation with the parents' own family doctor. In normal circumstances your own home provides a better environment for the birth to take place, if this is possible. There you are surrounded by your personal belongings and the baby can be put to sleep in its own cradle from the start. In your home certain decisions can be made and acted upon but which may be beyond your control if baby is delivered in a hospital. In some maternity hospitals, tiny babies in the nursery have been known to be subjected to loud voices, strident music from a radio, and noise from a television set in the ward lounge, as well as a great deal of disturbance from other people's visitors. This can be distressing to mothers and babies during a crucial time when peace and quiet should prevail. Mothers who are confined in hospital should, whenever possible, have their baby beside their bed, or in the same room as they are; at least then they know whose baby is screaming! It does not seem to occur to many hospital staff that the safest place a baby can possibly be is with its own mother, and in this connection we quote Dr Victor Bott:

> The cold, impersonal atmosphere of a maternity de-
> partment is indisputably just the opposite of what one
> would wish for. For the sake of convenience—what
> errors this leads us into—the newborn baby is isolated

from its mother when its right place is by her side. It needs the warmth of its mother—not only the physical warmth but the spiritual warmth of its mother's love. Since it is impossible to demonstrate this with the help of a thermometer, it is merely declared that it does not exist or that it is of no importance! It will one day be realized that the arbitrarily instituted measures of our day in consequence of our ignorance of true human nature will have their repercussions, not only on the mental state but also on the physical health, giving rise to conditions whose manifestations could have effect right up to old age.[6]

Why induction?

There are many reasons, some of which are important from a spiritual point of view, why birth should *not* be hastened or induced unless it is absolutely necessary for medical reasons, and not merely to suit the convenience of mother or medical staff. Dr Glas has the following to say in this respect:

> Before birth, the forces of the stars work on the form of the child while it is surrounded by the embryonic membranes and by the mother's body. After birth, having cast off its coverings, the newborn baby is exposed directly to these forces. The moment of birth is one of great importance for the child. It is a completely new situation, like the change from a bud to a blossom. Something new is being created. It is important to know that the individuality, in coming down to the parents, strives to be born under a constellation he or she has chosen.[7]

This of course has nothing to do with ordinary astrology, or 'reading one's stars' in a magazine or newspaper. Most people do not sufficiently understand that we are indeed cosmic as well as earthly beings, and that our very physical constitution, with its vital organs, is modelled on a heavenly scale. The many rhythms that are known to astronomers and physiologists alike may not be explicable in strictly materialistic terms, but may be explicable in spiritual terms. The subject is a vast one, and cannot be discussed in detail within the present context. Readers are referred to the Notes for one or two examples, together with a suggested reading list.[7]

The current tendency, common in the USA and now spreading to other countries, to employ Caesarian section when this is not strictly necessary—often in order to ensure a swift and crisis-free birth without complications for mother or child—is to be deplored. We are living in times which are very difficult for doctors and nurses because much of the so-called civilized world has caught the American way of dealing with awkward or difficult situations—by lawsuit. So now we have the scenario where a pregnant woman fully expects her baby to be perfect, and doctors, fearing the outcome of legal battles if anything untoward occurs during gestation or birth to damage the baby, are responding in ways that would never have been contemplated years ago. Babies are induced to suit the people involved—parents and/or doctor—and more babies than ever before are being born by Caesarian section, an operation which is not undertaken without certain unwelcome risks and results of its own. The fact that the baby is not 'caressed' by the muscles of the birth passage means that the baby born by Caesarian section is deprived of its first vital experience of sensory touch. Such a baby will need plenty of gentle stroking and warm hugs during its childhood to compensate for this. In a certain sense, the child so born will not have had to encounter the kind of 'opposition' supplied by the factor of pressure such as the child who is born naturally experiences in the form of resistance.

During the post-natal period, any mother's impatience to get back to work or 'get back to normal' is harmful and disturbing to future relationships with the baby. Do not harbour the expectation that life will be 'normal', for life will never be the same again! Many changes will have occurred in the mother's body during pregnancy, and will continue to do so after the baby is born. The process can be quite traumatic, especially for a new mother. Part of this trauma is the emotional reaction to the arrival of her baby. The intense love and joy gives way at times to anxiety and weepiness, even depression. The responsibilities of motherhood will weigh heavily upon every caring mother. Finding the new relationship with the baby may mean for some mothers a kind of crisis that can last up to the third month after the birth of her baby.[8] Dr Glas suggests that until she feels stronger in herself, every mother should remain quietly in bed for 10–14 days, or even longer if necessary, despite pressures to do otherwise. The internal organs need time to readjust themselves, and a calm, restful environment is necessary for this process to take place. Have a sleep yourself when baby is asleep, and catch up on all those necessary tasks later, when you are more rested.

And what about the hustle and bustle?

During pregnancy it is best for your health if you avoid too much rushing about. After your baby has been born, it will thrive better if it is not taken anywhere by car or public transport for the first *six* weeks, indeed, not even taken out of your house during this time. If your baby was born in hospital this is of course not possible, but always be conscious of those hazards of contemporary life which will shock your delicate and tender baby's constitution, for these will actually 'harden' the physical body faster than so-called normal. Where infants are involved, exactly the same principle applies, if this hardening-off process takes place too soon, as to tender plants. It is probable that sclerotic illness occurring in later life, such as rheumatism, arthritis, hardening of the arteries and suchlike, may be due to the practice of enforced maturation.

Before the baby is born, parents usually enjoy all the necessary forward planning, discussing where the baby will sleep, how its bedroom will be furnished and decorated, what name to give to baby, and so on. All too often this is done in the name of fashion rather than with the baby's true interests at heart. The choice of a child's name is a significant matter, and great care and sensitivity is necessary in view of the fact that it will be available for use—or misuse—from babyhood until old age. Few parents fully realize that a newborn baby is so sensitive to its environment that it can actually be harmed by its surroundings. Plain bedroom curtains in clear but muted pastel shades, free from 'busy' patterns and 'loud' colour schemes are preferable for baby's bedroom. It should not be exposed to curtains or wallpaper designs featuring a certain 'humanized mouse' or those featuring 'animalized people' or garish, futuristic themes. Equally inappropriate are designs that include humanized railway trains or stylized cars, aeroplanes or indeed any-thing which can be—and *will* be—studied repeatedly by a baby 'captive' in its cradle or cot, and later its bed.

Soften the harsh outlines of the world

A baby needs protection from any bright lights and harsh contours in its surroundings. Veils made from silk or fine muslin material hung around the baby's cradle to facilitate this are strongly recommended. A delicate light blue colour is very suitable, and a rose pink veil under a blue one is also very appropriate as the resulting colour is somewhat like that experienced by the foetus in the uterus. We know babies who have benefited very much from such veils having been draped around their cradle, and later their cot. They are relaxed and contented, sleep well and enjoy going to bed. A baby should never be placed in a position where it is facing the light, especially that from a sunny window. It is distressing to see how many tiny babies are fully exposed to bright sunlight from which they, prisoners in their prams and pushchairs, cannot escape. They squint and squirm unhappily, hardly able to avert their eyes, possibly unnoticed by their mothers who meanwhile have their eyes averted from the sun, or are perhaps wearing sun-glasses, untroubled by its blinding light. How forgiving of their carer's unthinking actions are such vulnerable, helpless children, and how uncomplaining they are in their trusting attitude!

Contrary to what child psychologists, magazine writers and baby 'experts' urge and advise, the baby should *not* be surrounded by 'stimulating' objects deliberately designed to develop precocity—that is, to 'foster its intellectual development'. The child must, as we repeat time and again, grow into the world *slowly*. Nobody in their right mind would seize a flower-bud and force open its petals in order to hasten its flowery character—would they? And so it is with your 'budding' human bundle of love. An infant's world is a dream world, and babies are very susceptible indeed to being startled and shocked by bright lights, sudden or loud noises or voices, by too much handling, and by being bundled from person to person, especially when 'new' to the world. None of us likes to be woken suddenly in the morning, as it takes time for us to become accustomed to surroundings even as familiar as our own bedroom; so imagine how a baby, with its dreamy consciousness, feels. It certainly needs a very long time to 'come to'.

The spiritual realities, Dr Glas observes, are that:

> The peaceful process of growth in the child undergoes a considerable change as the soul draws gradually into the body from birth onwards. This entry of the soul is accomplished upon a threefold path. Only two of the three gateways through which the soul is led into the body are open to our influence, namely, the way of

nutrition, and the way of the sense organs. The first is opened immediately after birth; it is that of the *breathing and circulation,* and is beyond our control. The breathing in of air forms the radical turning-point between continuous sleep during embryonic and foetal life and the awakening of consciousness.*

From the moment breathing starts, the baby can already give signs of its feeling life; it cries, and thereby indicates that the soul experiences with pain its entry into its physical home...The second is when the incarnating soul follows the path along which the food is carried through the organs of metabolism. The third road for the soul's entrance into the body is provided by the sense organs. These are directed outwards to the external world, and the nerves connected with them lead to the central nervous system.*9

As the very air which the baby breathes helps to mould and sculpt its organs, anything which shocks it—cold air, loud noises, arguing, nasty thoughts—will affect the rhythm and character of a baby's breathing and will cause damage or weakness to the organism, and this may not be apparent until an individual is in his or her forties or fifties. Breathing is a far more complex process than most people realize, and shock can be deduced from observation of the way it breathes—gasping and panting, holding its breath, heightening facial colour, involuntary waving of arms in the air, sudden shrieking or urgent, terrified crying or screaming, and a look of alarm in the eyes. It would be

---

* In these two processes can be observed the moment when the baby becomes *conscious.* The 'element' of air is traditionally associated with the astral principle. Consciousness, as mentioned elsewhere, is a function of the human astral body, which is served by the whole system of nerves and senses. In passing, it is interesting to note that it is nitrogen in particular that is connected with astrality, just as oxygen is associated with etheric forces. Carbon is represented in the solid physical-material body.

unrealistic to expect that infants and children remain unaffected by the rapid changes in attitudes within society over recent decades. Indeed, it must be admitted that very little is being done to protect them from what in modern life seems innocuous and harmless but is in reality insidious and detrimental to human existence itself. Certainly, the standards of health in both children and adults alike are falling steadily, and under present conditions will continue to do so, inevitably and inexorably.

Grasping situations

The baby slowly and gradually absorbs impressions of everything in its environment, as we have discussed elsewhere. It reaches out, as it were, and 'grasps' all it can see and feel, and pulls these impressions back within itself, literally internalizing them. Imagine what all this is like to a young child. For instance, stare for a few minutes at an object without taking in anything else in the vicinity, and then shut your eyes. The shape of that object will still be there, although dimmer and less distinct. You will remain unconscious of the real processes involved in the act of seeing, though conscious of what is actually seen. It is our ego which has the task of co-ordinating all sense-impressions almost automatically, and arriving at—and grasping—an instant comprehension of what is going on. This process lies at the basis of our experience of *shock*, of whatever magnitude.

If you recall how you feel on wakening, when you are neither asleep nor awake, and imagine how you would react if upon opening your eyes you are dazzled by a bright light, startled by a shrill noise, loud conversation, or other overwhelming sense-impression, then you will appreciate how 'shocking' these events are to a child when in a state of dream-consciousness prior to waking up. A child experiences such delightfully glorious dream-consciousness as normal during all its waking hours. That is why it needs a relatively featureless, unstimulating environment which does not wake it up too soon from its sublime, almost heavenly state, demanding its attention by sheer force of presence. Small wonder that an infant who is so rudely wrested from this enviable condition when woken up too soon, whatever the reason, is fractious and irritable.

Remember your child has chosen YOU!

It seems to a new mother, a new parent, that any freedom enjoyed hitherto, prior to the birth or even conception of the baby, has gone for ever. So many aspects of life become distorted even though some are temporary, such as a sort of memory loss, when the right word is hard to find, and the constant 'hearing' of the baby's crying—even when, upon checking, it is found not to be crying but asleep. No meal seems to go uninterrupted by the baby's crying or imagined crying, and throughout the day constant checking on the baby's breathing to see if it is still alive is nerve-wracking. When the baby cries, there is also the nervous strain of trying to determine *why* it is crying! However, upon reflection, many years later, these times may be looked back upon as some of the happiest in your life, and perhaps the most fulfilling.

> *...when I act in the presence of a child under seven, my action is not only my own concern but it directly affects the will-forces of the child. My behaviour is no longer my own affair, but all my deeds, my will, my feelings, all my thoughts and ideas, all work on as imponderables in the child. It makes all the difference in the world, whether I live near a child with a good and kindly attitude towards life and let the child grow up in such an atmosphere, or whether my attitude is selfish and inhibiting. Such imponderables are not yet generally recognized.*[10]
>
> Rudolf Steiner
> *The Renewal of Education*

3. Getting Priorities Right

A new-born child can be pictured in the following way. The little body, with its over-developed head — the younger the child the bigger in proportion to the rest of the body, is the head — this little body is surrounded by the invisible soul and spirit. As the child grows these latter are to find their way, step by step, to physical expression. The soul must gradually enter the body. Those around the child, then, should take care that nothing is over-hastened, nothing done by force, but all through real love.[1]

Norbert Glas
Conception, Birth and Early Childhood

Seeds of stress

At birth the child who has been protected from the outer world by maternal 'wrappings' is now thrust into the world, open to all possible hazards. After birth, remember, *everything is a shock to the baby*, even when it is carefully and lovingly handled. Nowadays, noise is insidious, all-pervading, and even polluting. As adults we have had to become hardened to it, and perhaps now suffer from tinnitus or deafness. But babies and young children are vulnerable in the extreme, for they are exposed in immediate reality to what we have had to get used to over decades. Later, we all suffer when the child does not prosper, when it is nervous, over-active, restless, hard of hearing, or 'highly-strung'. One of the major problems of our times is that far too many individuals do not feel wanted, do not feel at home in the world, and are liable many years later to depression, anxiety and nervous fatigue. Perhaps their crises began in the early hours of life, with insufficient warmth, and too much in the way of frightening, shocking noise and general over-stimulation of the senses. Suffering immeasurably from such irritations from birth and as they grow older, little children are now a very visible group in a stressed population.

You should always be able to get close enough to the baby in its cradle or bed in order to hear its delicate, almost imperceptible breathing. The new-born baby has been accustomed to a constant temperature of about 98°F within its mother during pregnancy, and at birth emerges into an ambient temperature of perhaps 75°F at most. After birth it must be kept warm, and the room in which your baby sleeps must also be warm, and free from draughts and sudden changes in temperature. Remember that a new-born baby is especially vulnerable to loss of body heat through its head. Too many mothers overlook the fact that the scanty hair covering provides little or no insulation, so do keep that cosy bonnet on! The fontanelle must be protected so that warmth is not lost through these openings in the skull-bones. Remember, too, that when a baby is warm it feels loved and wanted; love is 'soul-warmth'—the spiritual equivalent of actual warmth in terms of physics—and which indeed we *all* crave for and need.

Treatment on arrival

It is not appropriate, we believe, to have a child born into water. From a spiritual point of view, the baby has come down to earth, via its mother's physical body, having developed its own physical body within the uterus, and so to be born on earth means just that—not into water. Where possible, every mother should experience the birth as fully and consciously as possible. Pregnancy and the birth process are all seen to be worthwhile when your baby's first cry is heard, and your beautiful child is handed to you to hold, cuddle and put to the breast. Everything that is done should be done through a devoted love for the baby. Your baby will then feel wanted.

The skin of the new-born baby is covered with a greasy substance (vermix caseosa) and one of its functions is that of nourishment.[2] This can be of great help to the baby during the first few days, and if it is removed the baby is deprived of an important nutrient, and the skin becomes more exposed to the external influences of heat and cold. Dr Glas suggests that after birth, the child may be cleaned with a little warm vegetable oil where necessary, and this should be wiped off gently in such a way that the original grease remains.

A daily bath is not necessary

Bathing the baby does not have to be done each day; two or three baths a week are sufficient. On other days it should have a good wash only, for too many baths make a child nervous, and letting baby do too much kicking produces a similar effect. Remember, you are the one who is responsible for deciding these matters, and it is your task to guard your baby from experiences that may induce timidity and nervousness. Before putting your tender child in its bath, always check and test carefully the temperature of the water. *Never* leave a child alone in the bathroom when the water is running into the bath; many children have been badly scalded when reaching out and falling into a bath with hot water in it. And never leave a baby or small child in a bath on its own—just let that telephone or doorbell go on ringing!

Swaddling is sensible

Research has now confirmed what people have known throughout the ages, namely, that swaddled babies sleep more, cry less and spend more of their waking time actively alert than other babies.[3] A new-born baby needs its arms 'constrained' by a cot-sheet being carefully bound around it, so that it does not become alarmed and gasp for breath, as it will if it feels its unrestrained arms waving freely through space. It has had no experience yet of being free to move, and it is terrified by the experience, just as it is by any sudden movement. Just plonking the baby in its cot, 'putting it to bed' as you would an older child and hoping for the best, simply is not good enough.

The usual method of swaddling a baby is done by laying it on the bed on a cotton baby blanket, with its head above the edge of the blanket. Care must be taken to ensure that your baby's arms are in the foetal position, and held in to its chest before the blanket is folded around it, one side at a time. When baby is placed into its cradle, put it down to sleep on alternate sides each time in order that its head does not become misshapen, and each time take care that its little ear is flat, and not bent forward. The rhyme 'Morning, noon and night, place her (him) on the right' can be useful for remembering when to put the baby on the right side—putting it on the left side on all other occasions.

Once your baby is so placed, put another sheet or blanket gently over it, tucking it down firmly each side, making sure that it is folded under its feet also. This covering should be free of baby's cheek, not rubbing it, and needless to say it should not cover its face. Now baby should be comfortable and should not be able to move onto its face. For the first few weeks a sheet may be placed under the mattress of the cradle with the ends protruding each side of the mattress. Place your swaddled baby on its side on the mattress and then bring the sheet up and over the baby by taking the end of the sheet which is on the side of the cradle baby is facing, taking it across and tucking it down under the other side of the mattress, at baby's back. The end of the sheet behind baby is then gently but firmly taken across and tucked down under the side baby is facing, thus holding it firmly and securely. Eventually, baby's ever-more vigorous movements will enable it to work free of its wrappings, thus indicating that swaddling may no longer be necessary.

Not on its stomach, please!

Research into 'cot deaths' has shown that laying a baby on its stomach to sleep is not advisable, and is indeed putting it at risk. A young child's breathing is in any case inclined to be irregular, as Dr Glas explains: 'The rate is 40–50 breaths per minute in the newly born, and about 24 in a two-year-old. At five years old it is 20, and at nine years old reaches 18, the rate in adults.'[4]

It is important to remember that putting a baby on its stomach to rest or sleep may affect its breathing rhythms. Moreover, damage may be done to its vital organs because these have no protection from its rib-cage as in an adult, as its bones are still soft. It is probably not coincidental that nowadays we see many young people who have long, curved necks; and it springs to mind that perhaps they, as infants, were put down to sleep on their stomach. This practice has now fallen into disfavour, and presently there are far fewer babies who need to stretch and strain their necks; most babies breathe more freely and are altogether more contented as a result of lying on their back or on alternate sides.

What about those 'comforters'?

The practice of giving some kind of artificial teat 'comforter' to a baby and toddler should be avoided. However, when a baby sucks its thumb or a finger, or a piece of its blanket, it is enjoying its sense of touch, usually just as it is drifting off to sleep. It seems that a child who sucks a thumb, finger or cloth (sometimes stroking its cheek at the same time), foregoes this habit by the time it is about three years of age. Certainly, a healthy, happy child would never wish to appear before the world with a dummy in its mouth! It indicates a certain lack of liveliness in the child if it is sucking a dummy during the daytime, and when it is out of doors in particular. This may well be a silent cry for more affection from its carers. As they grow older, children usually take a keen interest in what is happening around them, for there is always something to do, and thumb-sucking habits are soon dropped. The question could be asked: when does a 'comforter' become a silencer? The origins of much adult unsociability may well lie with daytime dummy-sucking habits—especially if children with these are not customarily spoken to, as the comforter would thwart their efforts to make reply.

Even a tiny baby may find comfort in a 'doll', made from pure fleece wool that has been washed and carded and then formed into a firm ball no larger than the mother's breast. This is then covered in some plain pure silk material, a square of silk which is then fastened securely around the 'neck' of the doll (which is of course all head), the remainder of the square flowing down beneath the head when it is held up making up the 'body'. The square of material should be hemmed so that there is no danger from loose threads. This doll is placed close to the baby's mouth, and a sense of comfort is evident from this experience as the baby nuzzles its lips against the doll. As the baby grows it will enjoy the touch of the silk, and later be able to stroke and handle the loose material. This can be washed when necessary. Such a doll cannot harm the baby's perception of its world, or over-stimulate it as other 'toys' may do, as we mention later.

When your baby is older and is awake for longer periods during the day, it should not be left too long on its own. Do not hesitate to sing as you carry it about in your arms for a while, for rest assured that it will be appreciated beyond words! The use of front or back baby carriers is always to be deplored. Many osteopaths have spoken out about the damage that is done to the pelvic and hip areas of babies carried around in such apparatus. It may seem a good idea, but in the long term you may damage your growing child. Don't forget that your baby's developing bones are soft! Please do *not* be tempted to 'drape' or hang your baby over your arm—have a care for those delicate inner organs beneath that soft rib-cage! You may have seen the misery and pain mirrored on the face of a tiny infant being carried around with its parent's arm holding it around its soft, tender abdomen—head flopping forward and legs and feet dangling—with the consequent displacement and stretching of the vital internal organs. When picking up your baby support its head by placing your hand underneath it, and carry baby in a *horizontal* position until it is strong enough to hold its head up.

It is important to maintain your baby mainly in a horizontal position until it indicates that it is ready for establishing itself in an upright posture. That is to say, when it is awake and in a state of resting or perhaps 'taking in' its surroundings while lying down, please resist the temptation to prop it up in a chair, even when harnessed or supported by cushions. Remember that baby's head—and the all-important brain that it houses—is disproportionately heavy and large compared with the rest of the body, and this means that when in the upright posture its brain does not displace sufficient cerebro-spinal fluid to maintain optimum—and harmless—flotation in it. This circumstance and condition is only arrived at when the child indicates that it is ready for maintaining itself in the vertical, and that is when it starts, without any prompting or 'forcing', to *raise itself* from the crawling position to the walking position. This time is usually heralded by the child's persistence in reaching up to suitable items of domestic furniture in order to maintain this upright stance.[5]

No noise, please!—for baby's sake

We do not subscribe to the notion that a baby should become accustomed to as much noise as possible, by exposing it to the sounds of washing machines, vacuum cleaners, radio, TV and general hubbub, simply because it has to, sooner or later. Such 'wallpaper noise' as this turns many children into what can only be called non-listeners. During its first six weeks or so, when baby seems to be unconscious of much of what is happening, it is nevertheless being affected by its environment and everything that happens in it, as mentioned elsewhere. Gradually, it becomes slowly more conscious of its world, but premature 'hardening' to it should be avoided as far as possible. Such children hear the utterances of parents and teachers also as 'wallpaper noise', and as a result these children can be difficult to live with and control, whether at home or in class. Noise pollution is a serious problem which involves both socialization and education of children and adolescents who, immersed in a world of endless cacophany, are becoming increasingly alienated from other people.

So be sure to surround your baby with the utmost gentleness and tenderness. Be careful that the environment it grows into takes into account baby's extreme sensitivity. Provide low lighting, ensure that there is no noise or confusion, and talk in a soft, gentle voice. It is important always to speak clearly and distinctly, taking care to articulate and enunciate every word—so no baby talk, please! Even a little reflection will show that by doing so you are laying the foundations for a pupil who will also speak clearly—and spell correctly. Your voice will reassure your baby when you speak and sing softly to it. There will never be any judgement passed by your child on your performance! You may think that you cannot sing very well, but it is certainly music to your baby's ears. Until your child, like all children, gets critical of all the people around it at about nine or ten years of age, he or she will think you are a lovely and wonderful parent, which you will be, of course—as well as a great singer!

Exercises for the baby?

For some years now, enthusiastic people, caught up by the current craze for aerobics, gym work-outs and suchlike have advocated exercises for babies even from birth. Such 'fitness freaks' believe—mistakenly—that regular manipulative exercises will result in healthier, fitter babies who will be free from all sorts of problems in the future. However, such unnecessary exercises are damaging to the healthy development of any baby, who should be kept undisturbed and surrounded by warmth, love, and a calm and peaceful atmosphere. It's a day's work for them simply to *grow*, so leave them to it! Introducing children to arbitrary physical exercise is most undesirable from a spiritual point of view.

The incarnating spirit does not reach the skeleton until the age of puberty, and before this time any exercise for children should be mainly in the form of running games, ring games and suchlike, or simply playing. In particular, those ever-popular mini-trampolines should be entirely shunned, as the bones and cartilage of boys and girls before puberty are simply not sufficiently hardened to withstand the pressures induced by jumping—even onto elasticated platforms. The effects of mechanical movements such as these 'physical jerks', which serve no purpose, emerge as restlessness and superficiality in later life. Rudolf Steiner strongly advised against exercises for babies and small children which harden the soft physical body prematurely, thus leading to early sclerosis in terms of the bodily health, and materialism in terms of thinking.[6] He advised that all people both young and old should avoid sunbathing, as this destroys their etheric forces. Inveterate sunbathers, farmers and outdoor workers risk getting a hardened, weatherbeaten skin with wrinkles, and years later may well develop skin cancer. Remember that sunbathing ages the skin, and that this kind of 'tanning' also produces leather!

A hardening process is an ageing process

Another ageing process occurs when children under the age of about seven years are taken swimming in chlorinated water—and that means every bathing pool. The chlorine kills off the bacteria, but also damages sensitive skin and delicate eyes. There is also the risk of a baby or small child getting a chill as a result of exposure to cool or cold water while swimming, or shivering because their wet bodies are exposed to the wind or to draughts. Many children may be seen suffering from a 'cold' on a warm summer's day! So many ageing and hardening agents are present in all aspects of our lives nowadays, and it is difficult to appreciate fully the dangers these present to us all, but particularly children. Furthermore, food preservatives, particularly the nitrates and nitrites, harden the 'insides' of people. Forgive us for mentioning that undertakers have noticed that corpses do not decompose as quickly as they used to, due presumably to the preservatives in so many foods.

The vexed question of toilet training

Despite claims made by relations and friends about the early progress their child has made or is making with its toilet training, care should be taken not to introduce a young child to a potty too soon. A baby should never be held on or over a potty before it can sit up without effort by itself, and even then this is too early. Common sense should rule at all times. It is only when the infant is sufficiently conscious of its bodily processes, expressed in the natural feeling of 'wanting to go', that it is actually ready for being put on the potty. It is to be expected that an active, lively toddler will resent being so immobilized. And when such 'inactivity' is being made the subject of so much concern by grown-ups, their excessive interest in what 'passes' may not only create a morbid interest on the part of the child, but at the same time sow the seeds of the power of manipulation of adults later, when he or she wants to be rewarded. Such early training can certainly prove to be 'counter-productive' in more senses than one. Such premature 'disturbance in the life forces, the etheric forces of the child', Dr Glas suggests, may be one of the reasons why so many children suffer much later from enuresis or bedwetting.[7] A child is usually potty-trained by the age of about three years. If not, then is the time to start being concerned about it. But even then, do not overreact and make it self-conscious about it.

A human being grows up *slowly*

An animal does not have a childhood, and grows more or less quickly into the world, according to its species. An animal behaves through instinct, but the incarnating ego can learn only by degrees to think and reason, and make decisions appropriate to the current incarnation. Each one of us is enticed onto the earth in order to keep abreast of civilization. Much happens between one incarnation and the next for the majority of people, and it may be said that it is more necessary in modern times to learn far more than our ancestors ever needed to. In fact, children now need *even longer* to become fully socialized and educated in order more efficiently to digest what they absorb from their environment. The more quickly a child is thrust into the world, the more precocious it is and the more vulnerable it is to 'outside' influences. As mentioned elsewhere, the demands made on today's children in mainstream education by reason of excessively intellectual teaching methods is tantamount to robbing them of their very *life-forces*, and they become prematurely aged as a result.

More and more perceptive educationists and psychologists deplore the kind of 'robbing' of childhood that is rapidly becoming established as the modern norm. This fact is being recognized and acknowledged by other thinking adults and even sensible teenagers who, looking back to their childhood, realize too late that they too were so deprived. There are those people who chant, 'But they've got to live in the world, and must not be protected too much or they won't be able to cope with life ...' The evidence indicates that a child who is loved and wanted, who is guided gently but firmly by caring parents who oversee its progress slowly into the world, and who knows that it is here on earth to fulfil its destiny, *will* cope with life extremely well.

Love has been devalued

While parental love has always been held to be important for children, social scientists 'continue to fight shy of the concept of "mother-love", regarding it as unmeasurable, sentimental or both,' and this has been undervalued by practitioners in their daily attitudes to children and their families. This has been undervalued in their staff training procedures, suggests Mia Kellmer Pringle. Mother-love is not readily defined in scientific terms nor easily measurable: '... now widely accepted by "tender-minded" theorists and practitioners, its vagueness continues to arouse unease, even hostility, among the "tough-minded"; so much so that the word "love" either appears in quotation marks or other terms, such as "warmth" or "attachment" are substituted.'[8]

Throughout this book, we unashamedly use terms for that which is not measurable, or even readily defined in scientific terms—words such as love, warmth and imitation, sympathy and antipathy and even soul and spirit. The fact that scientists of some persuasions and disciplines cannot measure these qualities does not mean that they do not exist. How did anyone get on with their lives in pre-scientific times, prior to the fifteenth century or so, before objects and phenomenon were 'reasoned' about, hypothesized, estimated, measured and weighed, assessed and evaluated, and so on? Unschooled people in remote and 'uncivilized' communities may be more balanced in their emotional life than many individuals in our communities.

During the current technological revolution people are forced to endure intense competition for whatever work is available; some earn huge salaries and command an apparently docile but ambitious, nervous, anxious and apprehensive workforce. The idea of loving one's neighbour as oneself seems very old-fashioned nowadays, and somewhat naive perhaps, as people struggle to survive the stresses and strains encountered in their own lives. Religion has unwittingly caused many problems, for religious ideologies have separated nations and families, and has been the prime cause of endless wars and strife. Political ideologies have influenced people's outlook on life, but all ideologies collapse in time, some more quickly than others. It seems that the interpretation of Darwin's theories concerning evolution has become fact. 'Survival of the fittest' seems to have become an underlying premise guiding the way most people view their life in relation to others. Indeed, some employ it as the reason, and even justification, for using violence against other people! Another significant cliché which some go by is 'Do them before they do you ...' This is indisputably the talk of barbarians.

The golden rule 'Do unto others as you would have them do unto you' represents the essence of the twin and complementary notions of reincarnation and karma or self-created destiny which underpins every other notion expressed in this book. We all know that we should love our neighbours as ourself—but how many of us do? Those who come to the understanding that we are all 'God's children', interrelated, interdependent, and with our respective destinies inextricably interwined, may freely perform deeds expressible as *practical love—love in action.* It requires the possession of altruistic qualities of a high order and strength of character for an individual to bring to realization this perfectly reasonable moral precept.

Ideally, your child will grow into the world slowly, and your patience will be rewarded when your child has become a sensitive, thoughtful, caring adult who is physically and psychologically well-balanced enough to cope with the stresses and strains of life. Your dreaming baby will have gained an inner strength, and later a confidence and awareness which will help it survive and overcome much that is put in its path by an insensitive society. Your greatest task in life will probably be bringing up your child, this reincarnating human being whose destiny is entwined with your own, and this entails a tremendous commitment. Your sacrifices and hard work will bring blessings upon you—even if they are not seen clearly or fully realized at times!

> *Everything in the nature of joy and love centering upon the child from its immediate environment, plenishes the forces of the physical body, rendering it supple, plastic and amenable to formative influence. The more love and happiness we can ensure for children in this first period, the fewer the obstacles later in life when, as adults, from out of his or her consciousness soul and through the work of the ego, they are to become individuals freely associating with the world.*[9]
>
> Rudolf Steiner
> *Metamorphoses of the Soul*

4. Some Advice You May Not Need

If you consider the child as it first comes into the world, if you observe its physical form, its movements, its expressions, its crying, its baby talk and so on — you will get a picture which is chiefly of the human body. But this picture will only be complete if you relate it to the middle age, and old age of the human being. In middle age the human being is more predominately soul, and in old age he or she is more spiritual ... the feeling-willing of the child develops into the feeling-thinking of the old person.[1]

Rudolf Steiner
Study of Man

So tired!

We have already stressed the importance of calmness and patience during pregnancy and after your baby is born. Please choose never to argue or raise your voice within hearing distance of your baby. It doesn't know that you are tired and weary as a result of lack of sleep and your new responsibilities. We repeat: *do* have a sleep yourself during the day *when the baby is having its sleep*; and don't feel guilty, for you can catch up on necessary tasks later, when you are rested. Sympathetic understanding from those who are able to give it is usually appreciated by a mother when her baby is tiny, for few textbooks dwell on the unbelievable tiredness which is experienced within a few days of the baby's birth. The constant feed times, the nervous strain imposed by the unexpected behaviour of each baby that is born (for each individual must be understood anew), the incredible responsibility of caring for this precious, tiny human being, is always, always there.

Peace at any price?

Gradually, an infant recognizes its mother by way of her smell, voice, and habits of handling, her singing, her moods. A baby is indeed wholly sense organ in that, spongelike, it takes up everything in its vicinity—the sounds, movements, moods and thoughts, loving and unloving, of those around it. That is why it is unhealthy and harmful to any baby to be subjected to shouting or arguing, loud animated conversations and laughter, television, radio or videos, computers and other machines. There is much talk about 'sensory overload' nowadays, and this is certainly something that you, your baby, and everyone else in the household can do well without. Then your baby, blessed with caring parents, living in a tranquil environment with a regular rhythm to each day, will grow in strength and begin to take more notice of its parents' actions and responses. At about six weeks baby will smile, and this of course is a wonderful moment. Gradually, it will get used to other people, 'taking them in' in a series of long, unblinking stares. Encourage visitors to speak quietly in your baby's presence, because there is always the chance that it may be over-stimulated by too much attention, albeit of a well-meaning and loving nature.

Your daily rhythms will change as your baby stays awake for longer during the day and sleeps for longer periods during the night. A regular rhythm to the day is very helpful, and important to everyone's well-being. When your baby learns that it is going to be fed when it is hungry it will feel loved and wanted, and will trust as well as love you. As it grows its daily rhythms can be regulated to fit in with the family's routines. A child is certainly the centre of its own universe, but think hard before you allow it to rule the household.

A baby's crying, especially that of a new-born, is distressing to hear. At first it raises feelings of anxiety and even fear for its well-being, but you will soon become accustomed to its crying patterns, the *way* it cries, and why it cries. However, after the first few days a certain rhythm develops, and your baby will cry in different ways according to whether it is hungry, has a wet or soiled nappy, or is cold, lonely or frightened. Generally, a baby that is warm, dry, fed and loved will not cry as much as one who is not. Having said that, it seems fairly common for a baby to have a spell of crying during the day, and this may last for what seems like hours. Sometimes this 'spell' happens during the night, for a tiny baby has no consciousness of night and day, or time! If it continues to cry for a long time when put to bed, run through a checklist in your mind. Has your baby been fed enough? Has it dry, clean nappies? Is it warm and cosy? Is its bed well-aired, warm and dry? Is its tummy warm and covered (a chill can cause cramps and stomach pains)? Is it over-tired or over-stimulated? Have you had too many visitors, or are you yourself over-tired and overwrought? It is often the first-born child who suffers from being kept up too long, and the unmistakable signs of weariness such as yawning, eye-rubbing or crying may be overlooked until it is too late, and the child is screaming!

Why is your baby crying?

This can be a most difficult question to answer. A tiny baby is the least accessible of all to us. It possesses no intellectual powers; it is completely lacking in the faculties of reason, judgement and decision-making. It does exactly 'as it likes'; we have no control over it whatsoever. On the contrary, *baby controls our actions*. We are its slaves, for as we have said, it really is the centre of its own universe, and everything revolves around it. Its etheric or formative forces are still far from being 'reconciled' to the physical body it has acquired from its parents. Similarly, the infant's astral principle, which sustains its (growing) self-consciousness and feeling life, is also as yet unorganized, existing as it were like a cloud that envelopes it.[2] This is why baby's behaviour is of an 'inconsequential' nature, that is to say, mainly thoughtless and irresponsible. Its ego is faced with the enormous task of drawing the etheric and astral 'bodies' into the developing physical body, and this is a task that takes up the first 20 years of its new incarnation! From a spiritual point of view, a baby suffers enormously while becoming used to its physical vehicle. With this realization in mind, your baby needs to be regarded with real compassion, love and true self-denial, not merely sentimental love of the maudlin kind.

Crying and attention seeking

A baby's consciousness of day and night develops slowly with the development and establishment of routines. Make sure *you* get enough rest and peaceful relaxation with your baby during each day. A routine such as the following becomes second nature after some experience with a new-born infant. After its feed, baby needs to be burped, have its nappy changed, and to be warmly wrapped so that it can move its limbs while feeling secure. If it is comfortable in its clothes, with no pins sticking into it, or buttons, lace or decorative trimming irritating its skin, it is ready for bed. When baby is no longer relaxed and responsive to your conversation, and is rubbing its eyes and yawning, then is the time to put it to bed *before* it gets over-stimulated and over-tired. You will find that as the baby becomes more conscious of its surroundings it may prefer to be in its own home and may be upset if put down to sleep in someone else's.

Gradually, the incarnating ego awakens to its world and, finding plenty to entertain it, the child may form a habit of being reluctant to settle down to sleep, so stimulation of any kind should be avoided at such a time. Unsettled behaviour at bedtime that becomes habitual may well be the start of sleeping problems.

Certain strategies can be tried in order to ensure that the reciprocal power and powerlessness of baby and adult is regulated so that even at this young age baby learns that it cannot be the boss. Many battles of will and forbearance are lost or won at this stage. Allow the baby to cry for a little time. Then, if it does not settle, check its nappy without picking it up out of bed (thus raising its hopes for attention). Change the nappy if it is wet or soiled, and check to see if baby is blue around the mouth, as this can be a sign of its having wind. After carefully sitting it up while supporting its head with your hand under its chin, you may dislodge any wind without too much difficulty.

If, however, baby is screaming with pain and drawing its legs up to its stomach, check to see that it is warm, especially around its tummy. Colic is a very painful experience for a baby, so give a little cooled, boiled water from a baby's bottle, or a few drops at a time from a teaspoon, taking care that it doesn't choke or get a wet chest from the dribbled water. Place the teat or teaspoon on top of the tongue, and ensure that the spoon does not hurt the baby's tender gums and mouth. The range of Weleda remedies includes a most effective and safe baby colic remedy.[3] Check your management strategies if these measures do not work for you. Are you picking baby up the moment it cries, each time it cries? If so, baby will become over-tired and be very hard to settle. Avoid the creation of habits such as rocking your baby to sleep or carrying it around in your arms until it falls asleep. Be firm, for as we have insisted elsewhere, you are the adult who makes the decisions when your baby needs a sleep, not the baby.

There may even come a time when your baby will scream and cry for what seems like hours, night after night. This is the time when a phone call to someone you trust may be in order, someone who is understanding and knowledgable about the particular crisis you are going through and who can reassure and advise you. Healthy babies often go through this stage, but it does not last too long once a routine is established. It only *seems* to be never-ending at the time!

In these respects, the importance of establishing regular routines and rhythms in personal, domestic and other affairs cannot be overestimated. As discussed earlier, the factor of rhythm is fundamental to everything involving the *etheric forces*, whether manifesting in the kingdoms of nature or in the wide cosmic spaces. This means in practical terms that it is always advantageous to preserve a definite rhythm in whatever area of personal life you choose, for by so doing you are 'harnessing' the etheric forces to your—and everyone else's—benefit. A crude form of this is *habit*, whereby we tend to do certain regular tasks unthinkingly, almost mechanically. The intelligent deployment of rhythms in whatever sphere of life, and the avoidance of irregularities whenever possible, always has positive results in that the stress associated with chaotic conditions is less likely to arise. All this calls for a certain measure of self-discipline, but the ends certainly justify the means.

Goodnight rhythms

It appears that there are increasing numbers of small children who do not settle down to sleep at night, and many seem terrified to go to sleep. They do not want to be left alone, and demand attention in a variety of ways. We repeat: it really is important to have a routine for your child's day. A child needs a sleep during the day, even until it is three or four years of age. It is unwise to put it down to sleep too late in the afternoon as it may sleep too long and not be ready for bed at its usual bedtime. As in all routines, it is you who make the decisions, not your child! You decide when your toddler is to go to bed, which is sufficiently early for it to get twelve hours of sound sleep. For quite some time before bedtime, avoid over-stimulating your baby by rushing it around, playing with it, allowing it to watch television, or anything else that will disturb its inner calm. Too much liquid just before going to bed is not a good idea either, despite the 'I'm thirsty!' pleas.

When your child has been put into its well-aired, warm bed, take time out to sing to it. Remember that it will not judge you, but will take real delight in your singing! A suitable prayer may be said out loud, although an infant need not actually be taught to say it, as it will gradually learn the words anyway. Many a child would be comforted to learn that it has a Guardian Angel, which is with it at all times and protects it through the night. Ancient wisdom knew of such beings, and recent books are available for consultation.[4] A few thoughts indicating this may be given, such as: 'After I go out of the room you can talk to your Guardian Angel and say thank you to it for looking after you so well today.' After this has been done comes the hug and goodnight kiss, followed by, 'Sweet dreams! See you in the morning!' The reassurance that you will be there the next day, at its dawning, will be most comforting to your child.

Remember that your child was 'asleep'—in earthly terms, of course—in the spiritual world until comparatively recently. In a manner of speaking, we cannot 'teach' a child anything about its very recent home—the spiritual world itself! What is of importance, however, is that the child is able to take over into sleep what it has experienced during its waking hours.[5] This is why it is so very important that a child's daytime activities should be consistent with the influences it receives in terms of its calm, wholesome environment and loving solicitude from its parents and significant others. Proper imitation is absolutely vital to every child under the age of six or seven, and thereafter all kinds of activities which engage the *feelings and the will*. Gradually, the child will, by being subject to kindly authority and appropriate educational methodologies such as those Rudolf Steiner advocated, and propounded in *Steiner Education in Theory and Practice,* and *Education and Beyond,* become able to carry over in a wholesome way its experiences of daytime activities which are entirely health-giving. Later, as an adult, he or she will be able to metamorphose during sleep daytime experiences from which can be gained considerable benefit in soul-spiritual terms, the benefits of which can then be applied in practical waking life.[6]

The comfort of the known

So you have your little baby setting out on its life's journey, its spirit-filled ego struggling against the restrictions and constrictions of its physical body. Strictly speaking, as mentioned elsewhere, the individuality for which you are now responsible is just as 'old' as you yourself are! Whereas before it was a 'free spirit' since its death on earth and during its sojourn in the spiritual world, now it is held captive in a physical body and is subject to the laws of earth's gravity. It is a 'child' only in purely earthly terms! No wonder the baby cries with the pain of it all, although—fortunately, perhaps—it is not conscious of the whole incarnating process of adjusting to terrestrial conditions. Because it is 'still filled with the devotion that one develops in the spiritual world'[7] it is devoted to its mother, its father and all those who come into contact with it. It expects, howbeit unconsciously, to be wanted and loved. So don't disappoint!

During the first years of your baby's life, it will have the fundamental impulse, the completely unconscious mood, that the whole world is of a moral nature. That is why anything that disturbs its dreaming consciousness is a shock to it, irrespective of whether it is pleasurable to the adult. A person unfamiliar to the baby, such as a relative, friend or acquaintance whom you meet in the street or elsewhere, and who greets the baby enthusiastically, shocks and startles it. Watch the expression in any baby's eyes when it is being made much of by other people, and be sensitive to its reactions. Ideally, an adult should hold back the impulse to make a fuss of baby or toddler until it approaches him or her of its own volition; then it is ready to accept the other person.

Remember to make use of your own imagination, and speak pictorially, or tell little stories, invent situations, and so on. Children really enjoy hearing about their parents' childhood, over and over again. This requires a little practice, perhaps, but in time you will enjoy it while giving everyone a pleasant surprise. Teaching a child to recognize words, and reconstruct puzzles and learn scientific facts about things awakens them prematurely from their state of dreaming consciousness. This is why a slightly modified televison news programme which includes 'news' about faraway places with strange-sounding names is not only a waste of time but does nothing but confuse and bewilder the average child. Precocious children may 'benefit', but even they would be far better occupied outdoors or doing some kind of craft or hobby.

Sensory overload plus

Great care must be taken in choosing the baby's pram and pushchair. Again, it must be stressed that, as when choosing bedroom furnishings, it is preferable to choose a pram with a hood lining which is restful to the eyes, not in bright, busy colours or patterns. The pram should be long enough to allow for several months' growth, and it should have wheels large enough to cope with the bumps caused by uneven pavements and roads. Most important for the baby's well-being and peace of mind is that, whether in pram or pushchair, *it should face its mother or pusher,* so that it remains reassured by their presence and cheerful 'conversation'. It is especially disturbing to your baby if it is facing away from you in its pram or pushchair and is unable to see your familiar and comforting features. Imagine being moved along through a 'hostile' world in which *you* face legs, feet, and parts of people other than their faces, not to mention shopping bags, dogs, and other 'buggies'. These sights, loud noises and sudden distractions scare your baby, as will heated exchanges between parents or others in the vicinity—right down into its physical body. Imagine sitting in that uncomfortable pushchair, with your legs dangling down unsupported, for hours at a time, when you are desperate to lie down and rest, or sleep. Imagine being strapped into one of those tortuously constricting car seats for babies, also for hours at a time. A baby is not an inanimate doll or a tiny adult!

With its 'will-nature' predominant, every baby and toddler is seized by a kind of compulsion to *keep moving*. A healthy infant is endlessly twitching its fingers, waving its arms about, kicking and stretching, and obviously longing to be rolling, crawling, pulling itself upright, and getting 'into everything'. It is certainly not in a baby's nature to sit still, so don't expect it to. So many situations a baby finds itself in nowadays, from car seats and high chairs to supermarket trolleys, are contrary to its nature. Constrained or confined children who are not able to move freely and run about are *deprived* children, and likely to grow up to be weak-willed and lacking in initiative and courage.

A child sets its own developmental limits

An infant gradually recognizes those about it and smiles at about six weeks of age as we have mentioned elsewhere. At first it likes to be kept well wrapped in order to feel boundaries around its physical body. Within weeks it will move its limbs more vigorously, and free its arms from its swaddling shawl. Then it passes through the stages which include lifting its head, watching its moving hands, grasping a finger or a 'dolly' peg, lying on its tummy with its arms waving in a bird-like gesture, rolling over, pulling itself along on the floor, sitting up by itself, making babbling sounds, crawling and later walking. Your child should be talking in sentences by the time it is about three years of age, becoming more adept at handling articles, feeding itself, and getting to where it wants to go. A child's co-ordination improves apace, and by about six years or so it will be able to skip and hop, jump and run fast.

The importance of the development of correct co-ordination during the incarnation process is absolutely crucial. During their first seven years, as we know, children are creatures of *will*, which is always expressed as action, deed. This marks the development of their sensori-motor skills, and as we all know it is practice that makes perfect. Rudolf Steiner averred that children 'think with their fingers', and there is more than a passing relationship between the skills developed by movements by the limbs and senses such as sight and touch and the commensurate powers of thinking being simultaneously acquired. This is why children enjoy everything to do with movement, including co-ordinated limb movements, and this is one of the reasons why craft work forms such an important part in the Waldorf curriculum. Art and creative practical work in all its forms is of enormous benefit to the incarnating ego, which is so intensely engaged in mastering its earthly vehicles during infancy, childhood and adolescence. *Activity*, preferably of a useful nature, is the key-word.

We have made generalizations rather than state when such events come about, for we want to stress that your baby should *not* be encouraged to do anything prematurely through adult 'assistance' by way of interference. Your baby is best carried in a horizontal position until it is able to sit up by its own efforts. It should never be pulled up into a sitting position or lifted from the floor by its arms. The baby is right in its instincts when, without help or hindrance, it pulls itself up into a sitting position, and later a standing position, prior to taking its first steps and then walking. The ability to stand upright on both legs is a culmination of an untiring repetition of countless attempts to do so, and the exertion of a will-force of which we can form an idea only with difficulty, and of which very few adults would be capable. It should not be aided by enthusiastic family members or others anxious that baby shall exhibit precocious advances in development, thereby indicating how 'intelligent' it is. Baby equipment such as sloping car seat-chairs, bouncing swings, baby bouncers and baby-walkers are inappropriate and harmful to an infant's development, because these devices encourage the baby to do what it has not yet got the strength or physiological maturity to do.

Time and space to grow...

Development takes place in *time* as well as in *space*, and observable behaviour is not necessarily an indication of what is actually taking place in the inner world of a child or adult, as Steiner explains. A so-called naughty child is more lively and boisterous because it has a strong spirit, and its body is not a hindrance to it, as in the case of a quiet child. This knowledge can be a comfort to parents of a 'difficult' son or daughter, and later to caring teachers. It is only when we take a long-term, holistic view of a person's life that we come to realize how different from each other the various maturational stages are.

During the first three years a child is learning to master its body as it gradually grows and develops, and its ego takes an ever firmer grip. By the time a child is walking competently it is able to use its hands to explore its world. Consciousness of self has also progressed to the stage of saying 'I' instead of its own name and responding with a vehement 'No!' to practically everything said to it. The formation of its physical body is happening during a child's first seven years. Your child is building up its own body from the inherited 'model' that you, the parents, have provided for it to incarnate into. You have provided the physical body which is a model for the spiritual being to copy and develop during its first seven years. The evidence that this is happening is that the baby's features become more defined as it grows older, its awkward movements become less clumsy, and its physical body changes its formation until the rounded out baby and young child has developed a waist and has leaner arms and legs.

Avoid promoting independence too soon

Despite what well-intentioned psychologists suggest, it is not fitting to expect children to become independent as soon as possible, thereby developing precociously. It is a fact that most children are being deprived of their childhood, and society at large is suffering for this. A child worries if it has to make decisions, and subconsciously feels let down by its parents if adults have not the confidence and authority to tell it what is to be done. Young children expect adults to make decisions for them, and it is unbelievable that so many adults do not seem to realize this simple and so very obvious fact. Deeply rooted in child nature is the propensity to *look up to* adults with admiration for what they can do. Children take what parents and teachers say as simple truth, and trust them absolutely and implicitly. Furthermore, people who actually encourage children to choose for themselves are making a rod for their own—and indeed the children's— back for later on. In any case, children should not be burdened with making decisions, or in any way be responsible for them. We all find it somewhat burdensome, even stressful, to have to take decisions, and it is cowardly to inflict this burden on young, immature minds which are utterly lacking in powers of sound judgement.

It is also natural for children to 'test' their parents, to find out where the limits of behaviour are. If a child creates a fuss when told what to wear by its mother or carer, as even three-year-old children have been known to do, then it is the parent's place to deal firmly with the situation.

What is essential is that every child should be guided by a loving authority such as its mother, father, or significant other, who says, 'Today we have porridge for breakfast!' and who puts out the clothing, appropriate for the weather and occasion, for the child to wear—*without question*. As for bedtime, it's 'Time for bed!' and no hesitating, much less arguing, when the complaints start, which they certainly will. If you are consistent and firm in your resolve then you will win the initial skirmishes and be stronger to cope with the battles at a later date. They, unlike adults, have no idea about the realities of life, and when parents construe ordinary childish tantrums as decision-making, then they have little but sorrow and trouble in prospect. Nowadays, when nobody seems to trust anybody else, the lack of faith and confidence that is spreading throughout society is bound to have devastating effects on the up and coming generations.

It is certain that if children are left to make their own decisions, however trifling, then the foundations are being laid for adults who are vacillating, wavering in judgement, views, outlook and opinions. They will tend to be unsure of themselves, and will not know how to handle their affairs in time of difficulty, and will quail when faced with the ordinary trials and vicissitudes of life. Once given way to, children become tyrannical, demanding and thoroughly 'spoiled', a scenario which easily results in doctors' surgeries being full of people who 'need' pills for anxiety, depression, sleeplessness and, most of all perhaps, *stress.* Anxiety and tension in childhood often accumulate year on year, and it is not always appreciated, as we have said elsewhere, that the results of a particular course of action— or inaction—though not always immediately apparent will emerge during adulthood. Parents are increasingly apprehensive about what other people think of them as parents, but a practical, common-sense but loving approach made does much to remedy mistakes.

Parents who know their own mind, who are sure of themselves, who can think for themselves, do not have to seek continually for authoritarian 'experts', parenting magazines and television programmes and advertisers to make up their minds for them. They have the strength of will to resist being bullied by their child, at whatever age, and after careful thought and consultation with significant others in the child's life they will stand firm against any kind of manipulative tactics and strategies from a determined daughter or son. Children form friendships and fall out of favour one with another, and it is a wise parent who does not get too emotionally involved in childhood disagreements. Many a child has caused difficulties to adult interpersonal relationships because of its dramatic exaggerations or untruths.

Imitation as a formative force

Elsewhere we have explained that the baby gradually forms its immature, unformed physical organs by means of its supersensory etheric forces which permeate every cell in the body. However, it bears repetition that everything in its environment affects a young child and subsequently affects its physical health for good or ill. Every gesture, every movement of its father or mother, or anyone else in its presence, is accompanied by an answering experience within and throughout the inner organism of a child. All that takes place in its surroundings is imitated down to the finest detail. The child's facility of learning to speak depends entirely on this.[8] Perpetual shocks and unreasonable behaviour towards babies and children in their early years result in the kind of turmoil which expresses itself in the children's breathing and circulation of the blood. This means that the lungs, heart, and the whole vascular system are adversely affected by such a condition. Through the whole of their life individuals bear

within themselves the inner effects of perceiving an adult's
ill-temper when they were children.[9] We mention this in the
chapter on discipline.

You will realize how important it is for the child to have
the right environment to live into, and the great responsibility that every adult has to be worthy of *imitation*. Steiner is
well worth quoting on the matter:

> When we observe the faults in our children which
> develop in later life, we should be prompted to a
> little self-knowledge. All that happens in the child's
> environment expresses itself in the physical organ-
> ism—though in a subtle and delicate sense. Loving
> treatment while the child is learning to walk, truthful-
> ness while it learns to speak, clarity and precision as it
> begins to be able to think—all these qualities become a
> part of the bodily constitution.[10]

We make no judgements about child-care centres, but
leave you to consider whether your child's whole development may be adversely affected as a result of attending
an establishment where so many young children are together, and various minders, that each does not know
whom to imitate—their father, their mother, this or that
child, or this or that 'teacher'! Because a child absorbs the
outer gestures of those around it, and perceives their
inner mood, it will experience the fear, anxiety, loneliness,
contentment and peace of mind according to what may
be experienced by the adult at the time. All adults while
in the presence of any child therefore need to 'sacrifice'
themselves and their immediate needs, for the sake of that
child. Always bear in mind that the soul-spiritual principles
of every child attend it like a following cloud. The child
therefore inevitably absorbs all the influences proceeding
from the astral body and ego of those around it *directly*, even
if unconsciously.

Be aware of what you say

In a practical sense this also means that your child should not be burdened with adult concerns, including those which involve the child in question and other family members, or in discussion and debate about how it should be brought up. Consensus about these matters should be reached behind the scenes and *never* in front of a child. Matters which involve adult life, such as making plans for the future, illness, good or bad relationships with others, and so on, should not be discussed within the hearing of children, for adult worries weigh them down. Children who overhear conversations involving themselves are often worried out of all proportion to the importance of the particular affair. All children of present generations are naturally precocious and, far from being excessively encouraged and stimulated to 'progress' in school or college life, need to be slowed and steadied. Changes in society are rapid, and the demands made on individuals in the course of ordinary life are unsettling and bewildering. Stress is now a significant factor in modern life, and much of this is caused by people's inability to adapt to the continuous innovations and reforms in every sphere of life. This is why children should be educated in ways that encourage flexibility, resilience and pliancy in their thinking, and this is precisely what Steiner's educational philosophy and practice is aimed to instil into pupils.

Working with love for the task

Later, when a child is past the age and phase of imitation, it is a worthwhile experience for it to have responsibility for a pet and learn to put a living creature, dependent on others for its care, before himself or herself—feeding and grooming it, changing its bedding and so on. If it is the child's pet, *your child* should be responsible for its care and attention. The bonus of your child having to do the same tasks day after day, week in, week out, is that such regularly repeated actions *strengthen the will*, and that is always desirable for all parties concerned. If a child can be allocated a garden plot, however small, and encouraged and advised as appropriate and necessary, this is also good for the will. Similarly, it should be expected, as a matter of course, to keep its room reasonably clean and tidy for the same reason.

Learning self-control

The eldest in the family is often one who wants to get ahead in all sorts of ways and is usually the child who 'breaks its parents in'. The eldest child can therefore experience difficulties younger children in the family don't usually experience. The second child usually wants to catch its older sister or brother up, while learning from their mistakes. Several children in a family provide ample opportunities that help to 'knock the corners off' one another, even though this is a painful process for all concerned. A healthy child is full of energy and is always busy doing something—even if it means fighting with a sibling. It is no good letting yourself get annoyed with this, even though your patience is sorely tried. Having said that, however, such quarrelling should be supervised so that the adult must be aware of any hazards likely to endanger life and limb, and when necessary take firm and resolute action.

By way of review

It is by imitation that small children learn. If you hit and smack another, or throw objects at another person, so will the child. Aggressiveness and behavioural difficulties start in the home, and children who do not know how to control their feelings before adolescence will have to work much harder to gain self-discipline and inner calm later. Adults

who can accept a child for its own sake indicate unconsciously as well as in obvious ways how they regard it.
Children love their parents and want to appear favourable
in their eyes. Sometimes parents are severely tested by their
child as it grows older. With growing consciousness of self,
children ascertain whether they are loved and wanted, even
if their behaviour is at times inappropriate. Be sure and
make clear to them that it is their *behaviour* you disapprove
of—not them as individuals, *who may always rely on your love
and support.*

It is as a result of its parents' acceptance of it, no matter
what it does, that a child builds up its self-esteem and knows
that it is wanted and loved. We are not saying, however, that
its behaviour should not be modified and corrected. Until
about seven it learns how to behave, even to the point of
learning to say 'please' and 'thank you', from imitating what
you do and say. After a child is about seven years old you can
explain why it is not appropriate to do this or that, and give
it rules to abide by, suggesting when necessary what a better
way might be, and so on. In any case, consideration for
others should be a house rule. It doesn't take too long for a
teenager to telephone his or her parents and explain why
they may be unavoidably late. Such thoughtful and consid-
erate actions save a lot of lost sleep, heartache and anxiety
for parents who know how badly 'the other chap' drives.

People's attitude should be one of gratitude for children's
presence on earth, and of devotion towards them, so that
their path of development is cleared of obstacles and hin-
drances until well ready to become independent and a 'free'
human being. By this we mean that, at their coming of age at
21, individuals should be so balanced in their development
as well-integrated personalities as to be free to make decisions based on all the choices available to them, and without
excessive recourse to authority figures or authoritarian personalities. The emphasis upon such a right to decide for
oneself is that decisions may be taken with the welfare of

others in mind, so that they may be free in their inner as well as their outer world. Pressuring people by means of moral and emotional blackmail by overt and covert means is all too common nowadays. It is all too often a case of 'if you don't support my cause I'll beat you up'—and history is full of examples of that.

> *Hence, although from its birth onwards we may only look upon the child with physical eyes, we will all the time be conscious of the fact — 'this too is a continuation.' And we will not only look to what human existence experiences after death, i.e. to the spiritual continuation of the physical; but we will be conscious that the physical existence here is a continuation of the spiritual, and that we, through education, have to carry on what has hitherto been done by higher beings without our participation.*[11]

Rudolf Steiner
Study of Man

5. Is Your Baby Fashion-conscious?

This 'I', this ego, is not an abstraction as certain philosophers have conceived it to be, but an entity as real as are the physical body, the etheric body, and the astral body; it is the human spirit. *From it emanates that force which gives our organism its individual human form, the force which impels the child to stand upright, to speak and to think. Like the other bodies it works through a medium — warmth.*[1]

Victor Bott
Anthroposophical Medicine

Blood and fire

The temperature band marking the limits of heat and cold where the maintenance of human life is concerned is comparatively very narrow indeed. In every way, blood is vital to our very existence and, by tradition, is associated with the element of *fire*. From a spiritual-scientific point of view it is representative in the physical-material of the spirit-filled human ego, which so to speak 'lives' in the blood. If the ego is to fulfil its function to the optimum, then the blood—and of course the body—must be maintained at this ideal temperature. Excessive heat is just as inadvisable as excessive cold, so the problem exists in the summer as well as the winter.

Clothes for the new-born baby

A new-born baby needs to be dressed in soft, warm, easy-to-put-on gowns of the 'old-fashioned' variety. Such a gown allows the dresser to put the gown over baby's head easily and quickly, with a minimum of disturbance and distress. Some gowns are designed to wrap around the baby and be fastened with a tie. If the gown has buttons down the back or front, make sure that the buttons are tiny so that the baby does not get hurt by having to lie on them. Remember that a small baby cannot move itself about, or turn away from a source of discomfort, so you have to imagine how your baby feels in a certain situation. During nappy changes a gown can just be pushed back, and this also with the minimum of disturbance to baby. The skirt of a gown allows freedom of movement as baby increases its activity—especially that of kicking.

Clearly, this sort of clothing allows the person dressing and undressing baby easier access. At the same time, baby's delicate arms and legs are not manipulated as they need to be when a 'stretch 'n' grow' type of garment is put on or taken off. This is a painful experience from the baby's point of view, and the fact that such garments seem to stretch does not guarantee that they allow enough freedom for your baby's vigorous movements. Apart from that, the synthetic material they are made from feels cold to the touch, and a baby needs woollen bootees under such a garment in order to keep its feet warm. Any baby or child needs warm undergarments that allow complete coverage of their vital organs within.

A new-born baby needs soft cotton vests and vests made of a wool/silk mixture, or pure wool, and these should be long enough to be pulled right down over the nappies. It may need a cotton vest next to its skin with a wool and silk vest over the cotton vest. At no time should a baby have a bare stomach even on a hot day, because this gives rise to digestive problems and subsequent misery. *Do not forget* that the baby's circulatory system is not able to cope with changes of temperature as is that of a fit and energetic mother or carer. If brushed cotton or towelling nappies are used it is necessary to have a wool overnappy of flannel, or knitted pure wool pilch knickers of the old-fashioned sort. These keep the baby warm and reduce the risk of chills and kidney problems later.

Several changes of clothes

Several lightweight cardigans of pure wool are needed for a new baby, for the number of times a baby sicks up a little milk and has to be changed yet again are countless. As well as wearing two vests, one of cotton and one of wool, a gown and a cardigan, a baby may also need to be wrapped in a cotton or woollen shawl or baby rug while it is being nursed. There is little warmth in acrylic shawls or clothes made from acrylics. Again, common sense must be to the fore. If the baby has cold legs and feet, or cold hands, it needs to be checked to find out why it is cool or cold. Baby's complexion should not be blue, and the limbs also should not have a blue tinge or excessively red colour in winter because these indicate that the baby is cold or chilled. Observe its colour most carefully at all times, and feel its cheek with the back of your hand or tips of your fingers. Maybe it has kicked its woollen bootees off, or needs mittens because the air temperature is down.

No hat equals problems

Baby should also have a bonnet or helmet of warm material, because it is from the head that the child develops, strange as this may seem. Because body heat escapes through the head, a baby or child always needs some sort of covering in order to keep it, and therefore the body, warm. This is really important! So many little children can be seen with no covering on their heads in winter and summer. They have the finest of hair, if they have any hair at all, and so are vulnerable to any draughts of wind in all seasons of the year. The ears are then also affected, with problems developing sooner or later. Painful earaches are common among children, from those due to a common chill to the now widespread condition of 'glue ear', with all sorts of problems following on from having grommets inserted in their ears. The extremities, we repeat, need to be kept warm; hands and feet must be kept warm preferably through the wearing of woollen bootees and, if necessary, woollen mittens.

It is all too often forgotten that babies grow amazingly quickly during these early months, and are soon ready for a larger size of garment. It used to be that small babies were sensibly dressed in clothes made of wool, cotton or silk, or mixtures of these. With the arrival of washing machines wool became less popular because the agitator's action matted and shrank it and the garments were ruined. The clothes really needed to be washed by hand, in luke warm water, but many mothers found it easier to toss the clothes into the washing machine and hope for the best. Acrylics became a popular material for this very reason; they could be treated in this way without any ill effects except on the health of the baby.

Acrylics are now so well disguised that buyers are easily misled by the appearance and feel of material and yarn. Wool has a warm feel, a certain smell, and tiny fibres which stand out from the body of the material, whether wool yarn or cloth. Pure wool yarns and garments always carry the logo of the international wool-growers stating this, and this is a safeguard if there is any doubt. Otherwise, the percentages of wool and synthetic materials is usually stated on the label. Wool allows the skin to breathe and so regulates the body heat in a healthy way. Acrylics are not really warm in cool conditions; paradoxically, they may be too warm in hot weather, for the fibre does not breathe as does wool. Most synthetic materials cannot absorb moisture, so that they become uncomfortable to wear in certain atmospheric conditions. In really cold weather they are practically useless. In over-heated conditions the skin becomes wet with perspiration, and this leads to the obvious danger of chilling.

Children are not conscious of when to put on or take off clothing according to circumstances, and even teenagers, in our experience, need to be reminded! Any kind of elasticated synthetic material should certainly be avoided, as it inhibits circulation of air and can constrict limb movement. In particular, panties, briefs and similar garments are most comfortable when made from naturally absorbent fibres such as cotton. Most children are very vulnerable to peer pressures, for good or ill. We are all vulnerable to advertisers' wiles. They don't really care about your child—it's your money they're after! An adult can choose when to put on a jersey or cardigan or extra clothes, but a child cannot regulate consciously its own heat. It used to be said that if grandmother put on another cardigan, or another shawl around her shoulders, then put an extra one on the baby. And vice versa, if grandmother takes her cardigan off take one off the baby—using common sense of course. By now it will be apparent that we believe that there is no substitute for natural fibres for both children and adults. It is not only a matter of the effects on body temperature, but equally important is the development of the sense of touch. These days so many objects are made of cold, hard materials that chill and harden the sensitivities of children, and may be the root cause of irritability and insensitive behaviour in later life.

Decades later health may suffer

Small children who are unable to keep their body temperature constantly warm, and 'normal', risk circulation, breathing and kidney problems later—even decades later, for it is not yet fully realized that what happens at a certain time in a person's life may have repercussions years afterwards. These subsequent problems can include arthritic conditions, kidney problems and chest complaints, and even cancer, for cancer is a disease of the 'cold' —both outer and inner, physical and psychological—and heat may 'burn up' potential cancerous cells. There are certain problems in our time which many people are not conscious of, and these include feeling warm in our inner being, in our inner world, when in actual fact our bodily temperature is not so-called 'normal'. The test is that when the exposed skin is touched and felt consciously, and found to be cool or cold, another garment should be put on to bring the temperature up to normal. Don't forget those warm socks or woollen tights!

Check the way the garments are made

Great care must be taken in choosing bootees, socks, mittens and gloves, for there have been incidents reported to the press of loose threads in garments such as these being caught and wound around a baby's or toddler's toe or finger, resulting in severe and painful swelling. Until a child develops a waist it needs clothes which hang from its shoulders; otherwise, the clothes need to be tight enough to take purchase onto its protruding tummy, and so must harm the circulation and the internal organs. If the child wears braces on its shorts, trousers or skirt, or if these are made with adjustable straps, such clothes will be more comfortable and healthy for it than those with elasticised waistbands. Dungarees, overalls or coveralls are comfortable for any child to wear, for it needs to feel relaxed. Needless to say, it is important to choose footwear that is sturdy, and with room enough for the toes to spread naturally and without constraint be kept warm. The proper fitting of shoes for children of all ages is crucial. Cheap, flimsy, ill-fitting shoes can harm the still developing bones of the feet and ankles. Some sandals of the 'thong' variety can cause a child to trip and fall, apart from giving rise to feelings of insecurity and anxiety.

Natural materials feel good

Of course, very great care is needed to safeguard a child's health at all times. There have been fires in bedrooms as a result of a defective or unsafe heating device, and never assume that children will not touch or overturn the heater in a bedroom or other room. Nightclothes should be made from fire-retardant materials, and probably pyjamas are safer than nighties, if there is a fire or heater in any room a small child has access to. 'Made-to-sell' sleep-suits of brightly coloured material, manufacturers' scraps and off-cuts randomly put together, are quite inappropriate for young children because the combination of colours and designs may arouse them to the point where they become over-stimulated and hyperactive, and find it difficult to get to sleep.

Is your baby *really* fashion-conscious?

It is disturbing to see so many children's clothes made of denim, a material woven for the hardest wear, originally intended for workmen doing the toughest of manual labour! Advertisers promote expensive baby and children's clothing in colourful materials, and with zips, buttons, metal studs on the pockets as focal points—veritable straightjackets! Young children are creatures of will; they need to be active, and they should be encouraged to be active. A baby who is dressed in uncomfortable clothes will be unhappy and restless, unable to settle down to sleep, and will be fretful if its clothes are too tight, made of unsuitable material, with trimmings such as lace scratching its almost non-existent neck. Comfortable clothing will make it feel warm, secure and *wanted*!

The weight and thickness of the clothing should certainly be taken into account, for a small child may be weighed down by a chunky-knit jersey or cardigan rather than one made from three ply wool. The fabric used for making dresses, skirts, blouses, shirts and trousers needs to be fine in texture rather than coarse material for the same reason. Until the fine and delicate skin is 'hardened' through exposure to the weather during childhood years, it should not be rubbed, chafed and irritated by materials in ways that would not be noticed by an adult. The infant is not a little adult and should not be dressed as such. It is not appropriate for a child to wear clothes made in the manner of teenage fashions, or adult ones either, as manufacturers try to persuade us to do. Let the baby be a child for as long as it should and may.

Trendy clothes in psychedelic colours or in very dark shades may even adversely affect your child's behaviour. Any pattern that is very 'busy' with small or large repeated flowing patterns, or with bold or large picture-patches and 'doodles', will impinge upon the consciousness of the child as well as on the children playing alongside the wearer of such clothing. The reason for this is that their eyes recreate the patterns over and over again, as if they had hands that are reaching out and are actually drawing or tracing the lines and patterns over and over again. This is why any pattern chosen for clothes, wallpapers, curtains, carpets and furniture should not over-stimulate the eyes and inner being of the viewer. If this sounds strange, try looking for a time at any such pattern while consciously imagining a hand stretching out from your eyes and drawing and tracing, and recreating the pattern you are studying. An example of this, with regard to the effect on the 'inner' being of a person, is that of a patterned wallpaper which is mismatched where the strips adjoin. It can be very irritating and tiring to the eyes, which try desperately, over and over again, to match up the pattern correctly.

It is preferable for children to be dressed in quiet, pale colours, and this applies to the mother or carer also. Plain, unpatterned materials free from over-bright, 'busy' or swirling patterns are to be preferred. Dark and sombre colours are not suitable for adults to wear in the presence of babies and small children. One of the reasons for this is that until the child is about nine or ten years of age it is 'at one' with the world; it feels that the world is an extension of itself, and is therefore affected directly. It is still in a relatively dreaming state, and is best left to 'come to' gradually; any kind of shock, pleasant or unpleasant, is best avoided. The colour black, currently so popular even for children, is the last colour they should see around them. In this connection the psychological effects of colours is significant, and this is not fully appreciated. For example, lively, over-active children become more calm and tractable when dressed in red. The complementary, soothing, pacifying colour green is experienced in their inner nature and this may be observed by a perceptive adult. Conversely, a phlegmatic, relatively inactive child responds favourably to being dressed in green, whereas a melancholic one reacts to being dressed in blue, and a sanguine child in yellow or orange.[2]

The outer becomes the inner

Pictures stamped onto children's clothing are yet another form of visual pollution. Probably the most grotesque are those of mice, frogs, dinosaurs, ducks, teddy bears and other unnatural, bizarre, 'created' species. The cute, sweetly attractive and dinky animals dressed in human clothing and presented as human beings are also to be deplored. All these weird artefacts produce huge profits for franchise holders, and are made to sell rather than satisfy aesthetic tastes and uplift the human spirit. It seems that the truly human factor in civilization is being deliberately devalued and prostituted by commercial interests. Everywhere, human beings are being increasingly 'animalized', while people are desperately and agonizingly searching for their higher, truly spiritual natures. They long to love and be loved and appreciated as individuals who have something to offer the world, but our very humanity is being crushed under the weight of commercial interests that are dominated by the profit motive.

These comments may sound negative, but children are being swamped with trendy, 'designer' type clothes and the brightest and most hideous of toys, bought for them by kindly relatives and friends. Parents may not object because they do not want to offend the same friends and relatives. We are inundated with ugly, unwholesome toys, and garish, poster-like pictures applied to clothing for children, and now even for babies. The sheer volume of such bizarre images and messages that floods towards us via advertising and the popular media is insidious in the extreme. Piped 'musak', garish colours and contradictory messages of all kinds that pour in from all quarters simply cannot be conducive to peace and tranquillity in anyone's inner world. Elsewhere it has been mentioned how 'the outer' becomes absorbed through the eyes and is then 'taken into the body' and imprinted upon the inner world of each individual. There is so much that is ugly around us, so surely it is wise to encourage every child to like and admire what is aesthetically pleasing, and to love what is truly *human*.

> *... beauty is moral goodness, is really a simple truth. The only sin is ugliness, and if we believed this with all our being, all other activities of the human spirit could be left to take care of themselves. That is why I believe that art is much more significant than either economics or philosophy. It is the direct measure of Man's spiritual vision.*[3]
>
> Herbert Read
> *The Meaning of Art*

6. Food Matters

'Tis not the Bread that feeds us;
What feeds us in the Bread
Is God's eternal Word—
His Spirit and His Life.

Angelus Silesius

Off to a good start

The first impressions made on any baby last—for the rest of its life. At birth a baby is extremely sensitive to all that is going on around it. Although outwardly it appears passive and unaware, in reality it is at its peak of susceptibility; it is, as Rudolf Steiner put it, 'wholly sense-organ'. It should be treated with devotion and reverence, and have the very best in terms of tender loving care—and that includes nutrition.

Breast-feeding versus bottle-feeding

The baby should be put to the breast soon after birth; this not only 'bonds' the baby to its mother in a physical sense, but it assists the milk flow. The baby does not then need any artificial substitutes and gains enormous benefits from colostrum, the fluid that is secreted for a few days after the baby has been born, and which differs from milk in that it has a higher protein and anti-bodies content. No other food can give the baby such a good start in life, for it provides protection against gastric infections and is invaluable in every way. When it is to be fed it should be put to the breast rather than be given its first feed through a plastic or rubber teat which is thrust into its mouth. Easy access to a relatively fast-flowing liquid as its initial food can lead to a reluctance to work at sucking at the breast. Moreover, the temperature of its mother's milk is just right at all times.

During the first few months of a baby's life, mother's milk provides all the sustenance baby requires. Milk contains not only albumen, carbohydrates, fats and salts in an easily assimilated combination, but it also bears 'cosmic, planetary and lunar forces—which have already contributed to the building up of the child when it was still in its mother's womb'.[1] This statement may seem to be rather strange, but it must be borne in mind that we are *of the whole universe as well as in it*, and genuinely *holistic* philosophies take account of this. The earth may seem to be our home, but we are beings of and therefore part of as well as dwellers in the universe as well as on the earth. Thereby milk, a truly *universal* substance, provides a continuing connection between baby and mother, who provides her child with powers of resistance to illness, which enable it to build up further its organism and prevent it from 'hardening' too quickly as it incarnates. The embryo uses the plastic-formative forces of the mother's blood to build up its organs,[2] and after birth it continues to receive these forces in the milk. Milk is the intermediary element between heaven, with its creative forces, and earth with its solidifying forces and substances.

Ideally, a baby should be fed on its mother's milk for about six months. It is inappropriate from a spiritual point of view to breast-feed a child beyond seven or eight months of age, for by that age the baby needs food that is more 'earthly' than the 'heavenly' milk, so to speak. Children remain too much connected with the maternal hereditary forces, and they become over-dependent on these forces if they are not weaned until later than this. The incarnating process demands that a child 'makes itself at home' in its *own* organism; and the years from birth until the shedding of the 'milk teeth' marks this gradual progression.

Digestive upsets are a cause for concern

There are many digestive problems associated with the giving of processed milk or cow's milk to a young baby. Rudolf Steiner recommended donkey's milk for babies who are not breast-fed, though realizing perhaps that this particular food item is unlikely to be readily available! Goat's milk may be available instead. Fresh cow's milk, proportionately diluted, is suitable as a substitute if a mother cannot feed her baby herself, but genuinely fresh milk is difficult for most people to obtain these days. Ideally, the health of the cows should be good, and what they eat should be free from any trace of pesticides, antibiotics, stimulants and plants that taint the milk—sadly, a forlorn hope nowadays. Evidence is now available proving that the addition of vitamins to children's food can actually harm them. What is nutritious is food that is full of life-giving forces rather than what is promoted by the food manufacturing industry. Since the introduction of 'soya bean milk', which is not in any sense milk, many mothers, particularly those of vegetarian or vegan persuasion, have been tempted to give this to their children in the sincere belief that it is a suitable substitute for real milk (which of course it is not).

Don't be shy in asking for advice, and explain any worries you may have. A rhythm in feeding will develop if you are relaxed and not anxious and nervous. The greatest problem associated with feeding any baby by bottle is the time involved in preparing the food, sterilizing the bottles, heating them to the right temperature, obtaining a teat of a size that does not 'drown' the baby through choking, or cause it to become impatient and tired if the hole is too fine to allow the milk through at a suitable rate. And if the bottle is not ready on time, watch out! There will certainly be loud screams, for an infant's hunger is instant! Needless to say, mothers who breast-feed their baby are doing themselves as well as their baby an enormous favour, and this fact is being rediscovered. Their diet should comprise nothing but the best in every possible respect, for the foundations laid at this time are to last for a whole lifetime.

Dr Steiner asserted that milk has the effect of arousing the *will*, and the first indications of this are the fervour with which baby takes its mother's breast, with much twitching of hands and feet, and squirming body movements while feeding. It is at this time that baby starts developing use of its limbs, which in turn affects the development of its 'left' brain and 'right' brain in a balanced way. A bottle-fed baby habitually cradled by the carer's left arm is able to exercise its left hand exclusively while being fed, whereas a breast-fed baby is able to use both hands as a consequence of being put to the left and right breasts alternately. Nature knows how to educate the left brain and right brain in these early stages of an individual's life, appropriately balancing the brain's development as a result of physical movements and activity of the limbs!

A naturally fed baby should be better off than one fed with 'milk' substitutes which are not actually milk, and / or cows' milk which has been pasteurized and become almost entirely 'denatured'. We say 'should' because breast milk may have some contamination from present-day health hazards such as pesticides, and other toxic substances that have been ingested by its mother and stored in her body tissues. However, the tendency which has developed to breast-feed a child beyond nine months or so is not really good for the child, even if the mother can't bear to 'let go'. Breast milk is high in sugar and can affect the teeth of a two-year-old, and it does not have the nutritional properties required by a toddler who needs food that is more substantial. In consequence, normal development induced by properly introduced weaning is inhibited.

Will-full behaviour

By about three months the baby recognizes its parents, is becoming aware of its surroundings in some detail and is reacting to various sounds. At about four to five months of age it begins to try to grasp things that are held out to it. During this stage of the child's development the skull grows firmer and more formed, while the fontanelle grows smaller and the features take more shape. Its body takes on a more definite form, and there is a rosiness of the skin which indicates an all-round healthy condition; the ligaments become tighter, the muscles become more organized and the baby's movements become more controlled. A healthy baby enjoys zestful kicking and flexing, 'taking everything in' visually, and has healthy breathing, digestion and elimination rhythms.

As mentioned often elsewhere in this book, it is the *will* principle that is being optimally developed during the first seven years of life, and we are so organized as to be able to express will, *in the final analysis*, only by means of our limbs. This is why baby, although unconscious of it, is wholly 'will-being'; it cannot yet think or express its feelings by any other means than action. It is first and last a *doer*, and it is at this time that the foundations of a strong and effective will are laid for development later into a strong-willed, resolute individual. In other words, baby is developing its will-power through the exercise of its so-called sensori-motor skills, observable when it reaches for and grips an object or a finger held out to it. Toes, feet and legs are all active during waking time, particularly while baby is being fed. Its limbs when free are in continual movement, and this is outer indication that the will is *awake* in the limbs, although it is still *dreaming* in its feelings and *asleep* in its thinking. Infants are totally incapable of causative thinking in spite of what experimental psychologists claim, when they impute adult characteristics to infants—characteristics which are simply not there. Advice based on their findings is passed on to unwary parents who are beguiled and misled by well-meaning if intellectually orientated researchers.

Proper weaning is vital

After the sixth month, in addition to milk baby should be given a few teaspoonfuls of orange or tangerine juice several times a day from fruit ripened by the sun. The juice of freshly pressed fruit actually stimulates the forces of feeling, of inner perceptiveness.[3] Liquids containing synthetic vitamins and artificial flavourings should on no account be given—it has got to be the 'real thing'. Now, baby's mid-day meal may consist of cow's milk thickened with a suitable farinaceous food, and perhaps later with semolina. Gradually introduce baby to two more substantial meals a day, prepared from milk porridges and vegetable broths mixed with semolina, sago, rice or vermicelli.

Needless to say, all food—whether for infants, children or adults—should be of the very highest quality, and this means that fruit and vegetables should be really *fresh*. So dig up part of that unproductive lawn! Labels on all food packages amply repay close scrutiny before purchase, for the inclusion of certain ingredients (e.g. animal tissue fats in baby milk powder, and many other baby 'foods', sugar, salt and other 'taste-enhancers', not to mention iron, synthetic vitamins, and preservatives, particularly nitrites, nitrates, colourings and other mysterious 'E'-labelled ingredients) will surprise or even shock a perceptive, health-conscious shopper. Frozen foods, and those which have been bottled, tinned, or otherwise *preserved* or *processed* are usually of far more benefit to manufacturers than to consumers. The interests of the food manufacturing industry do not necessarily coincide with those of its customers, though it is heartening to see that many supermarkets have special departments for 'healthy' foods. Babies do not, as food advertisers would have us believe, get bored with bland foods, and common sense suggests that baby's meals should be lovingly and reverentially prepared by its devoted mother or carer—*for this there is no substitute*!

With this transition from the juice of 'sun' fruit to carbohydrates obtained from sun-ripened rather than artificially dried grain, and made into soups and thin porridges, a certain mineralizing process takes place through the cooking of the flour from the seeds of plants. This helps bring the child 'down to earth' slowly, just as it should do. Unrefined cane sugar as opposed to beet sugar helps to do this also, and so *cane* sugar is used for sweetening. Refined beet sugar is too closely connected with the earth and its mineralizing influences, and as such is inappropriate for infants who should not be exposed to such 'hardening' elements. Adults can cope with such a commodity, but in any case cane sugar is always preferable.

Nothing but the best!

The baby may soon proceed to having vegetable purées, such as *sieved* spinach, and red-gold carrots. It is inappropriate to give meat broth or meat to a child at this young age as meat 'connects mankind strongly to the earth forces and cuts human beings off from cosmic influences'.[4] The child at this age depends on these influences and is likely to become restless and nervous in later years if meat is given at this period of development. Ideally, meat should not be included in the diet of healthy children of any age, but especially before the child has completed its first year. Many children simply do not like meat, and strongly resist being pressurized into eating it; and in such a case their preferences should be taken into consideration and be respected.

Baby may also have *mashed* carrots, spinach and cauliflower after its first year, by the end of which its intake of milk should have been reduced to no more than a pint per day. So far we have discussed the child's food from birth: mother's milk up until about six months of infancy, then cow's milk, followed by fruit juice and vegetables, fruit or seed of cereals, then green leaves, then stems, and lastly roots with their essential mineral salts. After a child has been started on carbohydrates in the form of cereals and vegetables it may later have a small quantity of butter added to its cooked food, because this renders it more digestible. Arguments involving the whole controversy concerning dairy foods are not called for here; suffice it to say that our ancestors seem to have done very well on them.

Margarine is unsuitable for children, as this enormously overrated 'food' is little more than vegetable oil through which hydrogen gas has been bubbled in order to solidify it. Vegetable oils differ greatly in their intrinsic value as foodstuffs, but in general we contend that olive oil reigns supreme, closely followed by seed oils such as sunflower, safflower and sesame. Peanut oil, and oil from soya beans come at the very bottom of the list of preferences of discriminating dieticians, cooks and chefs—and for very good reasons. Just ask them why! Fat, in the form of butter, keeps the digestive system well enough 'oiled', and helps to prevent constipation and other ills. Crusts of bread may be given when baby is old enough to chew on them without choking, as the activity of chewing maintains the teeth in a healthy condition and promotes will-power as well. However, close supervision of the child while it is chewing on a crust and indeed during all feeding times is always necessary.

Is meat a dietary necessity?

Meat is animal tissue formed as the result of the ingestion of plant material and is therefore a 'pre-processed' foodstuff. By this very fact, it is in some ways an 'instant' food that requires less digestive effort in the sense of expenditure of *will*-forces on our part. (It is well known that the intestinal tracts of vegetarians are longer than those of meat-eaters.) The consumption by young and even older children of various 'luncheon' type meats preserved by chemical means, and meat and fish pastes, is to be deplored. These meats, and other foods containing preservatives, have a hardening effect on the organs of children and adults alike, but especially so on children. Meat pies, sausages, salami and similar foods high in preservatives and spices, and of rather dubious origin (ears, snouts, eyeballs, and worse!), always require careful forethought before purchase.

In real terms, therefore, meat-eaters are actually *weaker* in constitution than vegetarians, although this may not appear to be the case at first sight. Many people admit that meat 'weighs them down', and there is no doubt that vegetarians are often more physically active and mentally alert than omnivores. Rudolf Steiner, while not openly advocating vegetarianism, made the observation that meat-eaters are certainly disadvantaged, stating that they go through life as it were with one arm tied behind their back. Fanaticism is always to be deplored, and militants of one persuasion or another exhibit an equal lack of balance, for adults should of course be free to choose their own diets.

A special word about eggs

All fertilized eggs, whatever their origin, possess the same intrinsic purpose, namely, that of giving rise to procreation of the species. Even if they have not been so fertilized—and this is the case with practically every egg offered for sale in food markets—the basic structure obtains. They are not particularly suitable or desirable as food, regardless of what orthodox nutritionists maintain. Little known facts about eggs have been given by Dr Norbert Glas, which are interesting in every respect:

The connection between the development of the human

will, the metabolic-limb system and the food stream that penetrates into the organism shows the importance of the food that is given in the early years of childhood. Much will depend upon the substances chosen and their quality. Nothing should be given to a baby that it cannot fully digest; this may endanger the whole life of the will. Rudolf Steiner suggests ... through eating eggs in the first years, people can lose that natural instinct that they should have in later years for what is the right kind of food for them.[5]

He goes on to explain that the egg has not only its content of fairly concentrated protein, but also the living forces that have the power to form a chick. In the ordinary course of digestion the specific individual quality inherent in every foodstuff has to be digested and any food that is not broken down in the right way may cause damage. This breaking down of the concentrated protein and the living forces intended for the developing chick is 'asking too much of the child's digestion'. Damage done may be evident in allergies such as nettle-rash or asthma. In addition, owing to their sex hormone content, the giving of too many eggs may give rise to premature onset of puberty, and hence another undesirable form of growth acceleration.[6]

Children not so affected may still take harm in the finer processes of their metabolism, resulting in the loss of their natural instincts for the right foods in the right quantities, firstly in childhood and later as a grown-up. There is plenty of evidence to indicate to even a casual observer that this is undoubtedly the case. The popularity of 'weight-watching' clubs, the various diet regimes, fitness centres, jogging and so on indicates that all is not well. The growing incidences of anorexia nervosa and bulimia also point in the same direction. Add to all these problems the fact that what many people eat feeds but does not nourish. The loss of real health, vigour and stamina in children and young people, now

increasingly evident, will inexorably result in steadily de-
creasing standards of disease resistance and general
robustness in the coming generations, and this in a cumulative fashion. It is of the greatest importance that we all
become conscious of the issues involved in our everyday
eating habits, and adjust them accordingly.

The formation of eating habits

A fussy eater should be ignored rather than pestered, and
should not be given snacks between meals, much less chocolate, sweets, fizzy drinks and so on. A small amount of food
on a small plate rather than a large plate piled up will be
more likely to tempt a nervous eater. By the time a child is
about three years of age the amount of milk may be reduced
gradually to half a pint per day. Between the third and the
seventh year a child may be allowed to eat most kinds of
food taken by adults, with the exception of greasy foods,
eggs, wine and beer, meat, spices and mushrooms. A diet of
these foods produces nervous, restless human beings who
tend to asthma and all sorts of allergies, reports Dr Hauschka.[7]
She gives advice about the care of young children with
digestive problems, explaining that a stubborn case of constipation can be helped by taking fruit acids, such as orange,
tangerine or raspberry juice, and 'blossom' products such as
raw cane sugar, honey or malt. Older children and adults
could benefit from eating prunes and/or figs.

All these foods can be used to stimulate the 'inner motility
proper to the metabolism', as they possess activating powers which ease the tendency to intestinal blocking and have
a synthesizing, moderating effect on the action of the liver.
(Don't forget that the humble prune works wonders!) The
metabolic processes become more fluid under their influence. Where an opposite, loose condition occurs, liver action
can be stimulated by the formative element inherent in
protein. Protein-fortified milk or strained rice-gruel can be

given to babies with diarrhoea, while older children benefit from arrowroot and rice—all of which pass only very slowly through the intestines.

Every child's diet should be planned with love and imagination, and not reduced to a rigid schedule. Children do not always like the kind of food they are offered, but a little of new foods or those they profess to dislike can be added to what they actually prefer. It is most important that a young child be guided and encouraged to overcome its food dislikes, so that a balance in eating habits gradually develops. A sensible management of children's diets can prevent family disputes at mealtimes, eating disorders in teenagers, and other maladies in later life. It is far kinder to a child to help it overcome its initial reluctance to try various foods and to develop the capacity to digest these than weakly give in to the child's whims. A child develops courage by facing challenges of the unknown, and coming to grips with them. At mealtimes an atmosphere of respect and even reverence should be cultivated consciously and deliberately, so as to instil in children an attitude of gratitude and appreciation for the food provided.

A child enjoys a structure to its day and regular routines in its everyday life, especially with regard to its meals. It is actually easier to have meals ready in anticipation of those yells of hunger than put up with them while you are preparing it. When your child is able to digest solids it will be most receptive to adult help when sitting on its carer's knee, despite the temptation to place it in a high-chair (which is tantamount to isolation from the family). As imitation is paramount during this time, a child will taste new foods more willingly when it has first a tiny taste of the food that is being eaten by its parents. It will learn to be flexible in its approach to trying new foods, and so not be a fussy eater. Snacks in between meals inhibit a child's appetite, and so too many extras between meals may create problems involving eating which may last for many years, even to becoming a 'food fad' when adult. Little children know when they have had enough to eat, and there will be a sound instinct behind their refusal of food if they have been fed sensibly. Once satisfied with what it enjoys eating a child will discard the rest, and trying to force any child to eat more than it is able to enjoy is unwise. A word of warning: a baby put down to rest with a bottle of sweetened drink or even fruit juice is at serious risk of tooth decay.

Recapitulatory overview

A healthy baby has usually doubled its birth weight by the age of five months, by twelve months has trebled it, and by the end of its second year it should weigh about four times its birth weight. A sensible, well-balanced diet of freshly prepared vegetables and fruit provides nourishment for children without the need for supplementary vitamins contained in fish oils, denatured cereals and fruit drinks, or synthetic vitamin tablets. Research into children's development in Britain has revealed that children who have been dosed with vitamin tablets in order to enhance their learning capacity have actually been harmed by this 'treatment', and they became ill. Remember: it can be dangerous to 'overdose' on vitamin supplements and tablets. It could be considered anti-social for anyone to become faddy in their eating by sticking to a diet once the acute stage of any illness is over, and food should be of the quality and variety that stimulates each individual's particular well-being.

Meals should be served at regular times. Those partaking of the meal should sit down while eating it rather than consuming it while standing up or moving about, for sitting down while eating the food helps the stomach's reception of the food and aids digestion. Buffet-style meals can only be regarded as unbecoming to civilized living. Mealtimes provide opportunities for members of a family to join in the sacrament of dining, sitting quietly without constant idle chatter, and certainly without conflict and 'bad' thoughts. All food offered to the diners should be of the very best quality in terms of freshness and purity; that is to say, free from artificial fertilizers, pesticides, hormones, preservatives and artificial additives in the form of flavour enhancers, such as monosodium glutamate, and colouring agents. Simple and natural vegetables grown by organic or biodynamic methods and processes are tasty and health-giving. The artistic setting out of the meal on dishes and on the table stimulates the digestive juices and helps to enhance the feelings of enjoyment and well-being during and after the meal.

Instant, convenient—and junk

One of the 'horror' stories of this decade immediately before the new century is that of the eating habits of many children, who nibble and poke at so-called junk food—potato crisps, sweet concoctions of chocolate and suchlike—and who quaff cans of Coke. It would seem that prefer-ence shown by many British children for 'chips with everything' is matched only by their yearning for baked beans with everything. These constitute 'main' meals for thousands of children who eat no vegetables, and precious little in the way of fresh fruit. No matter how delicious the chips and tasty the baked beans, imbalances are bound to occur in the metabolic system, to the great delight and profit of the manufacturers of pimple-preventing creams and remedies. It is no wonder that so many children are pale, generally unhealthy, and lacking will-power. Many people are undernourished, and this is quite evident in the lack of vitality made apparent by their dull, muddy com-plexion and lack of 'bloom', and their general lassitude. The 'Take five' campaign, by which we are all encouraged to include at least five different *fresh* fruits and / or vegetables in our daily diet, is entirely laudable, as are the various government crusades against excessive consumption of sugar, fats and salt.

So-called convenience foods, when eaten in excess, serve to cripple, harm and even wreck the physical health of millions of human beings who are destroying themselves through neglect or ignorance, or both. Even those people who would not confess to being gullible have little chance against the unrelenting enticements of advertisements and special offers. The invention of the micro-wave oven was a very mixed blessing indeed. Apart from high frequency radiation 'leakage' hazards, cases of food poisoning as the result of eating only partly cooked food are all too common. In any case, re-heated food of any kind is undesirable from every point of view, as are those ever-popular 'take-away' foods of various kinds.

Food as a sacrament

The saying of a grace or prayer before meals is not a common practice these days. A grace is at the same time a meditation, and when uttered it helps to place each human being fairly in his or her place. The rhythms of the seasons, the phases of the moon and the movements of the sun, together with the four elements of heat, air, water and earth, do in very truth provide us with the nourishment we need to sustain us in our daily tasks. We really should be 'duly grateful', but the casual attitudes prevalent towards most things in our modern society now include our food, clothing and general manners and customs. Food is regarded as a 'consumer product' just like any other, and most foods have been processed and/or packaged in ways that conceal their original appearance.

Nowadays, consumers are far removed, in time as well as space, from the origins of most foodstuffs. The gardener, who with care and patience tends his seedlings and crops, spending time and effort in doing so, is likely to have far more respect for food than the average supermarket shopper.

All this notwithstanding, it is vitally important to bring to our consciousness the fact that it is the food we eat that provides a bridge between the physical-material and the soul-spiritual. It is not merely a source of energy and produced by the 'combustion' of foodstuffs in the 'furnace' of our digestive system, as orthodox physiologists would have us believe. There are mysteries connected with the processes of nourishment that have yet to be revealed, and modern nutritionists are gradually making these known. These secrets were known to our ancestors, who realized that matter has its origins in spirit and acknowledged this in their obeisances. A glimpse of their attitude is apparent in the grace which follows.

> *Sun, Earth and air*
> *Have wrought, by God's care*
> *That the plants live and bear.*
> *Praising God for this food*
> *In Truth live, we would,*
> *And bear Beauty and Good.*

7. From Play to Work

The impulse for activity, the urge to do something, lies at the basis of human nature, in the adult as in the child. The external world demands of the adult finished work, and is often harsh in its demands. Evolving human nature in the child demands an appropriate activity which, when rightly introduced and guided, forms an initial seed of future work. In its play the child is earnest and sincere in its activity, and this is a manifestation of the universal human urge for deeds.[1]

Gilbert Childs
Steiner Education in Theory and Practice

Play is a serious business

Play for a child involves movement and activity. Although such activity may seem to an adult to be a trivial mimicking of adult activities, it is a very serious business to a child—who is of course creating its own world through play. Unfortunately, however, adult entrepreneurs have carefully devised numerous and varied 'games' and 'toys' for children in order to make money—a lot of money! These have been carefully thought out by adults in order to catch the child's attention, thereby creating a desire within the child (or adult) for these various gimmicky, usually brightly coloured and trendy toys. Since the material that was initially called plastic, because of its quality of being easily moulded into shape, arrived on the scene, cheaper toys have been flooding the market.

Taking objects apart to see what is happening inside is natural to any child, but many children delight in smashing things up and discarding them without thought, for they are seldom worth mending (even if this were possible). If left unchecked such behaviour may give rise to further vandalism or destructiveness in later life. Subconsciously, a child develops an attitude of contempt for such playthings. It learns not to value objects that can easily and cheaply be replaced; and as it grows older its expectations develop and change, and a taste for more expensive toys develops. Children have never needed such toys, because even nowadays they are happy playing with natural materials when provided with these and encouraged to use them. Bean seeds can be most attractive to children (when past the age of putting them in their mouth, nose or ears) and they can be put together to make farm fences and gates, houses and so on. Stones, shells, seeds, cones, wood off-cuts, tree branches, twigs, leaves and flowers can be arranged in ways beyond most adults' imagination, and continue to stimulate and exercise any child's fantasy.

Rigid playthings lead to rigid thinking

Plastic toys are usually cold to the touch, and there is generally a brittleness about the material; the toy may soon break, disappointment and frustration results, and so more toys are needed to replace the losses. It is a grand way to learn about our throwaway society from a very young age, and a splendid preparation for becoming a consumer of the cookers, refrigerators, cars and so on that are not made to last more than a few years. Picture a child who, filled with delight when given a toy, is shocked within its inner being when that object breaks or falls apart, and the initial delight and joy quickly turns to dismay and anger. The very word 'plastic', which was originally used for describing the *properties* of a material or substance that was pliable and therefore able to be shaped or formed, is now used for the product *resulting* from such a moulding process. Here we have an interesting notion, one that is essentially paradoxical and contradictory. 'Plastic' toys are made from material which is *not* in any way flexible in the sense that it can be re-formed, or metamorphosed into something new. It is, on the contrary, rigid and 'unplastic', unless heated, firm to the touch and unchanging in its properties under normal conditions, and usually feels unvaryingly the same to the child's sensitive fingertips and developing sense of touch. The plastic toys, rattles, cups, plates and other artefacts that are given to a baby to hold and suck are harmful to its development.

We in society are actually surrounding the children with ugliness *as a principle*. Grotesque and bizarre 'playthings' that are the stuff of nightmares greatly outnumber the wholesome toys of even a decade or so ago. We wonder whether there is a connection between the number and severity of crimes, including those of violence in all its forms—towards other people, including helpless babies and elderly folk, and even animals. Does 'ugly' behaviour have its foundations in the many subtle lies and misrepresentations that we see created all around us, from humanized animals to the lies perpetrated every minute of the day and night via our television sets? Truth, Beauty and Goodness are basics which we need to understand and recognize in every aspect of society.

It is through play that a child develops habits for work, and these habits are formed for better or worse during the early years. During play the child learns many sensorimotor and co-ordination skills. Children should learn how to treat tools and other articles that have been used during their play with respect, putting these away after use. It is during this phase of their life that children learn to pick up and put away objects, and thus social skills involving responsibility for one's own actions are inculcated. This takes time and patience, but in the long term everyone benefits. A caring, kind mother who wants to 'help' by tidying everything up after it is not assisting her child to

learn how to share tasks and be responsible for its belongings, as later a flatmate, wife or husband will testify.

Stimulating imagination

During childhood a child needs guidance and protection
from that which is ugly in design and appearance so that it
may have toys and activities which help to develop rightly
its soul or feeling faculties. Mechanical activities such as
putting together cubes from boxes of 'bricks' limit the imagination, as does any arbitrary shape, even if it appears that a
child can 'create' something itself from the blocks and
interlocking shapes so popular today. They have an atomiz-
ing and fragmenting effect, and desolate a person. A doll
which has any mechanism to make it move or 'speak' is
positively harmful.[2] It is a lie in a very profound sense, for
human beings are not mechanisms, and the child is consciously and subconsciously bewildered because of such
lies. A beautiful doll with fixed features prevents a child
from unfolding its imagination. It does not let the child's
creative faculties grow. Steiner suggests that:

> However strongly we may suggest to children that they
> ought to love such toys—the forces of their uncon-
> scious and subconscious life are stronger, and they
> have an intense antipathy to anything resembling the
> beautiful doll. For, as I will show you, such toys really
> amount to an inner punishment...An inner, formative
> force is at work in the child. All that comes to it from the
> environment passes over into its being and there be-
> comes an inner formative power, a power that also
> builds up the organs of the body...the child is perpetu-
> ally at work as a kind of inner sculptor upon its own
> being. If we give the child the kind of doll made from a
> handkerchief (with two spots for eyes), these plastic,
> creative forces that arise in the human organism—

especially from the rhythmic system of the breathing and blood circulation—build up the brain, flow gently upwards towards the brain. They mould the brain like a sculptor who works upon his material with a fine and supple hand—a hand permeated with the forces of soul and spirit. Everything here is in a formative process, in organic development. The child looks at the hand-kerchief-doll and there becomes formative force, which then flows upwards from the rhythmic system and works upon the structure of the brain.

If, on the contrary, we give the child one of the so-called 'beautiful' dolls which can move, which has moving eyes and painted cheeks, real hair, and so on—a hideous, ghastly production from the artistic point of view—then the plastic, brain-building forces that are generated in the rhythmic system have the effect of constant lashes of a whip. The child cannot as yet understand these things and it is as though the brain were enduring the lashings of a whip. The brain is thoroughly whipped, thoroughly flogged in a fearful way.

Such is the secret of the 'beautiful' doll, and it can be applied to many of the playthings given to the child today...If the child's brain has been flogged in the way I have described, permanent injury is done to the soul.[3]

Since Dr Steiner spoke these words the most fearsome, ugly, mechanistic 'toys' have been produced and promoted. We repeat: there is a continuing stream of evil-looking, grotesque and bizarre toys which shock by their ugliness and distortions of face and body. The imprinting of these onto the 'unconscious and subconscious' of a child may well bear some kind of 'fruit' in the future—whether in the form of assault and murder, rape, or destruction of property. We suggest that by means of these toys, and over-intellectual educational methods, adults are 'vandalizing' the souls of children. To quote Rudolf Steiner again: 'There is nothing wrong with the children. It is the grown-ups who are wrong. We need not talk about how we should manage the children, but should rather begin to understand how to manage ourselves ...'[4]

Adults devise 'play' activities and equipment as a result of intellectual concepts based on what they believe is happening within a baby and small child. Their theories and beliefs are fairly firmly based on scientific research entrenched in materialism rather than on a knowledge of the human being gained from spiritual-scientific research. A baby stretching out to touch a plastic object on a baby-gym, or on an A-frame above it, is reaching out for an object that bears no relation to anything in its 'real' life, and this is in effect as harmful as the fully formed toy. Its senses are being bombarded all the time; it cannot look away, or escape, if it cannot yet crawl by itself. It is in every way a torture. Such objects are *not needed* by a baby. They stimulate the senses prematurely, impair and damage the imagination, and harden the physical body accordingly.

Babies do not get bored

Toys therefore are *not* needed by a baby until it is several months old because it will initially entertain itself by looking at its fingers and hands before progressing to reaching out and touching things. It will not get bored—that is an adult problem. Natural wooden toys which are not painted in bright, over-stimulating colours with garish designs are best. Wood is 'warm' to the touch, and its natural grain with its flowing patterns is attractive and intriguing. At first objects such as a wooden 'dolly' peg, a wooden rattle, a wooden teething ring and suchlike should be light enough for baby to handle. Before a baby can move about the floor it will enjoy handling simple and safe wooden toys. Always check that these are free from sharp edges and splinters.

A child of a few months old may be given a doll which is quite large, made from a natural material such as cotton interlock, and stuffed with pure, clean, carded, cosy fleece wool. The doll will have rudimentary limbs, and ideally be left without features, or have mere dots for eyes and mouth, so that the child itself can provide the features through imaginative play. Such a doll can then be seen 'crying' or 'smiling' according to the child's free fantasy. Permanently 'fixed' features cannot allow of this, and so thwarts free play of fancy and inventiveness. Little children will be happy with a doll which has clothes (but attached to its body), or even have a sort of 'bag body', as if it is enclosed in a sleeping bag. Detailed instructions for making suitable dolls in variety are readily found in specialist books.[5]

A new world for baby

Once able to move about on the floor, your baby will enjoy touching new-found objects, furniture and so on. Everything breakable should be put well out of reach, for despite what some adults believe a small child cannot think rationally as an adult does. It is earnestly exploring and experiencing the world around it and *cannot think in terms of cause and effect*: 'If I knock that glass vase against the table it will break,' will never enter its mind. Psychologists all too frequently assume that a baby is capable of thinking like an adult, ascribing to it powers of logical thinking which it does not yet possess. They impute their own ways and habits of thinking to children, and their advice can be positively harmful because it is—superficially at any rate—so plausible. They seem not to be able to differentiate between precocity and ordinary sound human development. The *urge to interfere* seems to be quite irresistible, but is understandable when matters of career advancement are involved.

The employment by psychologists of 'verbal definitions'

and jargon is deliberate and conditioned by their academic training, and is intended to impress and even intimidate 'lay' opinion—effectively undermining ordinary common sense. Their influence via parenting magazines and television programmes, not to mention teacher training courses, is for the most part far too strong. They gleefully quote the latest—the very latest—experimental work, which is then peddled enthusiastically until that next very latest research data from some 'classic experiment' or other appears. Current terms such as 'social referencing' and 'stranger anxiety' express concepts which every mother soon acquires—but from practical experience. And statements such as 'babies are *programmed* to seek attention', and 'babies are *designed* to protect themselves' unwittingly betray the mechanistic philosophies behind modern psychological thinking.

Orthodox child psychologists are sincere when they urge parents to stimulate their child's imagination; this is right and good. Unwittingly, however, they are harming and hindering the very children they are so earnestly trying to help realize their potential. In effect and in fact, the 'stimulation' they advocate is of the *wrong kind*. But tragically, they do not know or understand that a child's imagination and potential intelligence is stimulated by toys and other playthings that are *unformed,* made from natural materials and free from adult-contrived, garish embellishments. It bears repetition that playthings should express the essential 'gesture' that is integral to their very crudeness of shape, thus leaving the child's creatively fertile imagination to 'complete' them. This is the principle that underlies the methodologies of class teachers in all Steiner schools.[6]

As Rudolf Steiner explains so carefully and clearly, the children's formative forces are stimulated to work upon the formation of the brain when they create their own world which includes such playthings as we have detailed. Every child, no matter what its sex, needs a doll to cuddle and hug.

How can boys learn parenting skills if they have not had this initial experience with loving their own 'baby' at the most formative period in their lives? We consider it high time that the ridiculously unbalanced claims associated with the 'gender problem' are challenged. This issue is of their own creation, and their arguments are dangerously ill-considered in relation to life-long education for children. The whole matter is tied up with one of their most firmly held principles, namely, that of *discrimination*. Boys are being discriminated against, and girls even more so! Nowadays, parents are encouraged to be 'politically correct' in issues of upbringing and socialization, in that dolls and similar 'decadent' and 'sexist' playthings should be shunned. In the case of many young mothers their first baby is in very truth their first doll.

Moving toys for toddlers

When baby is walking unaided it may in addition be given simple wooden animal toys which can be pulled along, and constructed so as to make some kind of additional movement, such as flapping wings, wagging tails, opening and closing of jaws, and so on. Small trolleys, carts and wheelbarrows give endless pleasure, and children are able to genuinely work with these, by fetching and carrying small objects for mother or father. These should be formed so that the 'gesture' and shape of the animal is present, but they should not appear *too* lifelike. It is at this very early age that the foundations for creative thinking and so-called lateral or divergent thinking are laid. *This fact is of tremendous importance and cannot be emphasized enough.* Once insightful, sensitive and perceptive parents realize and implement these suggestions, and understand the rationale underpinning them, they will have made a great step forward in terms of understanding their child's mental and physical development.

It is all too often that a child's bedroom is cluttered up with toys bought by loving parents, and adoring friends and relations. Too many toys in a room, scattered about, can lead to a kind of wearied confusion and bewilderment on the child's part and irritation for the parent, with the result that both become scattered rather than centred and in harmony. Any cupboard which baby is allowed to open may contain surprise items, and makeshift toys and 'interesting' objects that are easy to handle and bang together. These are always most pleasurable to a baby even if the noise disturbs you! Otherwise, cupboards should be made inaccessible to a baby who is constantly on the move during its explorations. It goes without saying that wall sockets, plugs and electrical leads, kettles, portable heaters and so on are always sources of potential danger to an active child. Once an infant can pull itself up unaided it may be necessary to keep the toilet door shut, for a lavatory pan is a most interesting place in which to splash hands, throw objects into, including yards of unravelled toilet paper.

Those awful 'comic' characters!

Caricatures of animals such as mice, ducks, dogs and other creatures should be avoided because they have lost 'all those soul-qualities that belong to every animal'.[7] Puppets and animated cartoons which are caricatures of animals are often quite grotesque and are products of adult inventiveness and wittiness, which is presumptuous anyway and insulting to the dignity of the innocent animals. The monkey and the bear are animals which are not appropriate to be reproduced for toys. There will be cries of outrage and scorn from many people over this statement, but it must be said. The monkey is 'a caricature of man when he is hardened in his being' and the bear is 'too strongly connected with the earth'.[8] Perhaps it would not be too absurd to suggest that

much of the materialistic thinking and emotional depriva-
tion evident in people in Britain is connected with their
obsession with the teddy bear in all its forms—even to the
point of bears with 'angel' wings hovering above flowers on
greetings cards. The child should be able to develop life in its
imagination, and not be held back from the spirit. Dr Glas,
an expert on the interpretation of fairy-tales, explains that
bears usually represent enchanted princes who have to be
redeemed from their earthly heaviness. His words are worth
repeating:

> With just this heaviness, the child should not unite
> himself at any early age. No toy animals at all should be
> given to the child before he is able to walk. It is much
> more important for him to watch people who have
> already achieved what he has to learn to become an
> upright walking creature. It is striking to see the way
> children watch the walking of adults before they can
> walk themselves. They never tire of looking at the feet
> of the grown-ups who are going about them. With the
> searching gaze of a scientist, they try to find out how it
> is that people are able to move about.[9]

Toy animals, picture books with illustrations of animals,
greeting cards with illustrations of animals wearing clothes
are *not* suitable. Animals are not human beings, they do not
wear clothes in their natural state and the trend to bring
human characteristics to all manner of animate beings and
inanimate objects must be viewed with alarm. This is yet
another way to degrade, dehumanize and ridicule the human being. As we mention elsewhere, a jigsaw puzzle
should never have pictures of human beings which are 'cut
through' to fit in the puzzle—from a child's point of view,
this is shocking and alarming. This is quite evident, as we
have experienced, for when two children saw an unfinished
doll's head being unwrapped from a cloth prior to work
on it being resumed, the distress of the boys was very

evident when they gasped in horror. The head of the doll was as real to them as the head of a baby. The human being is 'divine' in the eyes of a young child, and for a child to see images of human beings cut into pieces is a terrible inner experience. Again, from a subconcious point of view, it is hard to estimate the damage this sort of thing is doing to a child's perception of other people. We certainly have had in Britain a number of murderers who have dismembered their victims in various appalling ways, as well as cats, dogs and horses being attacked with knives and other sharp instruments.

Some of the old-fashioned toys are making a comeback, which is good news. These include collapsible and moving toys which show people and animals doing certain activities such as men sawing wood or doing somersaults, chickens pecking at 'grain' on the ground, and similar. There are others but if these cannot be found in shops there are manuals available complete with designs to copy. Dolls for older children may be made from natural materials also, but variations can be made which are suitable for older rather than younger children. These dolls can have removable clothes which should include undergarments such as a child would wear. In all 'play' the real world should be reflected. The dolls may have long hair which is suitable to plait and do up in a variety of styles. This type of doll may have a suggestion of a nose and dots for eyes and mouth. Older children love finger puppets, and should be encouraged to invent and retell suitable stories to each other while moving the characters on their fingers. There are books available which give instructions for finger games and these are always popular, especially when rhymes are sung or spoken at the same time as the actions are done. As already suggested, natural materials such as tree branches, large seeds, teasels, shells and irregularly shaped pieces of wood are suitable for a child to construct and reconstruct towers, houses, buildings, farms, fences and so on during play. During such activities, children will work at devising various situations without the need for adult interference.

Repetition is important

A child will invent games which it needs for its own development. It will climb up a bank, fall down and laugh and try again and again until it succeeds. The same will-power is evident in a child climbing up the steps to the slide, and it will slide down and then repeat the performance over and over again. Hide-and-seek is a favourite game. A small child looks with great anticipation and will laugh with great glee when someone hides behind something and then reappears. If a basket is provided a child will love collecting up various items and give them one by one to someone else. This activity can be repeated time and time again.

Activities such as finger knitting and simple sewing are very suitable for children older than about three years. There are many activities suitable for children to help with while learning useful skills. These can include sanding wood and learning to hold a hammer and hit nails with it. They usually love to help with the gardening, soon learning how to use a garden trowel and dig the soil, and will willingly fetch and carry tools, push the wheelbarrow and collect up the weeds. Supervised activities imitated from adult work is always well worth while because every child looks forward to growing up to be like its parents or grandparents who work with enthusiasm. This is the whole object and purpose of growing up! Even dusting the furniture and sweeping the floor should be done with great care and in a gentle, unhurried manner in front of the child, and this is absorbed and later recreated in a similar loving and careful manner. Washing dishes and drying dishes is an important skill to learn. A child needs to learn that there is a place for everything and that everything should be in its place after use.

Play is work

As we suggested earlier, a child is learning purposeful activity when it 'plays' in preparation for adult life. It learns that hands and fingers are able to do and make things for other people, and that when it grows up it will be able to work like 'big' people do. It used to be that a grandparent would have the time and skills to show a child how to make things and do 'work' for others. An aunt or elderly friend may have the time and patience to show a child how to knit (a useful skill for boys also) and crochet, and embroider an ovencloth or something useful and practical. Whatever is done with the child should be done with enthusiasm and love for the task, for these attitudes complemented by feelings of gratitude are important attributes for one's well-being later in life, even into old age. Remember the old adage: *Laborare est orare* — to work is to pray.

On a warm summer day a child just loves to play with a bucket of water and a bucket of sand out in the garden. If you have no garden, a day at the beach or a holiday at the beach is just wonderful! Children enjoy playing with water, and love making mud pies and decorating these with flower heads, seed heads and grass. It is wonderful to be able to have a small patch of dug garden in which to create a river and a dam in the soil, and rebuild and recreate the waterway. No plastic apparatus, however cleverly designed and made by an adult, can take the place of the continually changing environment in the garden, where a child can create a garden, a river, a lake, or just enjoy the mud on hands and fingers and between the toes. Children learn that they can change things and make them new, and to accept responsibility and credit for what they have done. Children who are able to be free to enjoy wholeheartedly such activities are very fortunate—never mind the dirt!

Trees in the garden suitable to climb or even build a hut in are a real bonus to those already fortunate enough to have room to run about freely and safely. A nearby park where they can enjoy swings, slides, climbing frames and so on under the eyes of a careful parent or carer is a welcome substitute.

Art for a child

A child of about two years of age loves to use crayons. The pleasure is in the movement and seeing the results of the movement forming on the paper in colour and lines, as the crayon goes round and round or back and forth; there is no inside or outside, no inner or outer, at this stage. It is not just a scribbling to a child while it is creating what is on the paper. Asking a child what it has drawn turns the pleasurable activity into an intellectual exercise, for the child has not consciously thought out what it is going to draw. *Please, don't ever ask your child what it has painted or drawn,* for this is not being fair. You could take time to admire the lovely colours, though!

At around about three years a child will form a circle with great concentration, forming an inside and an outside. Within the circle is drawn a dot or a cross and this is an indication that what is happening in the inner world of the child is being expressed in the outer. This is the first indication of the appearance of a true ego-sense, of being able to differentiate between self and not-self. All children are unconscious of this, needless to say. Many an adult artist can tell clearly that what is seen and experienced in the outer world is imaged in the inner world, and is later given outer form through artistic work such as painting or drawing. This is not a copying of nature directly, but a re-creation through imagination of what has been experienced, consciously and unconsciously, in the environment.

Every picture tells a story

Children's inner development and the way in which it is manifested is expressed in their drawings and paintings, as the weeks and months go by. The ego, invisible to the senses, is thus revealed in its true nature, and the manner in which it 'descends' into the child's constitution can be traced by reference to children's drawings and paintings whatever their race and nationality. Thus their inner and outer development can be seen to develop in parallel.[10] The first indications appear when a circular form is drawn, which is representative of the child's outer form, its earthly home, as it were. Later, at about the age of three years, the 'I' motif is added, which is shown as a cross or star that radiates from within the circle outwards.

Audrey McAllen explains that the various forms indicating the incarnating process are produced unconsciously, and are universal symbols: the square with patterns arranged within, the birds in the sky, the ladder with a face at the top, the railway track, the armless 'child' with hair radiating out and a dot in the centre of the body circle. Extended arms are then added to the round body, and the hands are formed as circles from which fingers also radiate. As the child matures, it draws its body as a more substantial structure in a picture of a house, which may first take the form of a circle inside which is drawn a vague shape of a child. Later, drawings of archetypal or 'universal' houses will each have straight sides and a pointed roof, and the child is shown within the house. Later, houses have chimneys added, with smoke coming out of them; then windows and doors are added, and eventually the inside of the house is drawn in. By the age of six or seven the full body image will appear beneath the arch of a rainbow.

There are of course other significant symbols which represent the incarnation process, regardless of the culture into which each particular child is born. This is true *self*-expression. It must be borne in mind, however, that these stages and phases are not necessarily expressed in their sequence or in their entirety, for so much depends on the opportunities of doing so; and in all this a sound and healthy upbringing is essential. An adult watching a child who is drawing or painting should pay close attention without comment or interference, and observe how completely the little artist is absorbed in its work. Silence should prevail, and each child left free from obtrusive, distracting comments or conversation with other children or adults watching over them.

It is fair to say that most people regard the first 'primitive' attempts at self-expression through drawing as meaningless and random, but this is far from being the case. Every stroke different children make on their paper with pencil or crayon *has meaning and significance for them personally*. In other words, they are doing no other than *communicating* with whatever constititutes their environment—parents and family, home and its setting—everything they are at the same time *imitating*. They are, in effect, saying something about what they are *experiencing and perceiving inwardly*, and the whole process is of tremendous importance and signficance. It is now that their actual bodily constitution is being formed for better or worse.

Some of these processes are vividly described by Audrey McAllen with reference to this particular stage in a child's development:

> Next to appear in his drawing are the boundaries of 'above' and 'below', a line of blue sky at the top of the paper, and a line of green or brown at the bottom; other scribbles, more meangingful for him than for us, still dance freely on the page. But the time comes when the house has found the site it stands on, and an awareness

of symmetry enters the drawing; flowers appear on each side of the house; it is flanked left and right by a tree; maybe there are two houses. It is now time for us to stop merely admiring his prowess as an artist and ask ourselves what he is doing, what he is showing us quite unconsciously in this first visual work of his. The numbers of objects, flowers, trees, lawns and pathways are indeed reproductions of the essential structure of his own body which he feels through its craftman's tools of hands, fingers, feet and toes! The last stage of this growing awareness of space, and his place in it, is his ability to express the movement of 'forward' and 'backward'. Just watch him make a rainbow shine over his house, watch him drawing the curve of its arc![11]

Outer noises stifle inner quiet

Children in these times are having difficulty reaching an inner equilibrium due to every manner of noise and distraction, and a lack of structure and rhythm in their day, week and year. They may need to be transported by bus or car if they live a distance from their local amenities. Parents may take their children in the car, because they feel they will be safer with them rather than walking to school or the shops, until they are much older and able to fend for themselves. Children and adults are often fearful of known and even unthought of hazards. We all live in a climate of fear exacerbated by the news and programmes on the radio and television, while other problems in the community are increasingly wittingly and unwittingly thrust on us. There are many people who do not like children, even their own, and this is creating a society with a decided lack of concern and sensitivity towards them. This general irritation and dislike of children is developing nervous, precocious children who are being 'awakened' to the world about them too early. Their childhood is being stolen from them. All these developing trends are worrying and deplorable, yet they are there.

Is sport such a good thing?

In an effort further to develop competitive traits, schoolchildren are being compelled to take part in sports designed to encourage the competitive spirit in the belief that this will be transferred later to successful business practice. More time is being allocated by schools to 'competitive' sports and games, regardless of the possible, and probable, escalation of the doubtful advantages involved in experiencing the polarities of success and failure—success, that is, for a few individuals compared with the failure of the 'vast majority'. Many children hate sports and many have had their tendons, knee joints, neck and spine vertebrae and discs and other organs seriously damaged for life at a most vulnerable time of physical and emotional development. Rahima Baldwin mentions:

> Steiner made two recommendations that aren't going to win him any points with parents today. He recommended that children avoid ballet and soccer. In ballet the fixed and artificial positions are foreign to the fluid and changing nature of the growing child. And ballet affects the same kind of vital energy involved in growth and reproduction, as evidenced by the high rate of menstrual irregularities in professional ballerinas. The discipline and fixed positions of ballet are very different from the rhythmical movement which Steiner recommends for 'dancing with children'. In soccer the exclusive use of the feet and the head in hitting the ball puts undue emphasis on the extremities at a time when the grade-school child is centred in the middle sphere, the heart/lung area.[12]

The human body, regarded by our forefathers as the

temple of the spirit, should not be abused as if it were a tool or instrument. In soccer the human head, which is sacred in many cultures, is put to the utterly barbaric use as an implement for hitting, much as a bat is employed to hit a ball. The human skull was fashioned specifically for protecting our most sensitive organ of all—our jelly-like brain. The violence towards other human beings in the shape of 'professional' fouls, scrums and tackles is seen to be done in the name of sport and 'fair play'(!) on rugby and soccer pitches everywhere. Although this may satisfy the need of 'real men' or even some women to show themselves off as such while entertaining the general public, it is still a hazardous pastime and certainly inappropriate for schoolchildren.

The kindergarten—a social milieu

Education starts in the home, and later socialization occurs for better or worse in a pre-school institution, such as a kindergarten, before formal intellectual school work is given. A kindergarten, a garden for children, rather than a 'nursery school', may provide a social milieu for young children to learn how to share and co-operate with others. Until a child is about three and a half years old it is attached to its mother or carer and that person is the one a child is bonded to as though by an invisible band. At about this age a child can gradually become accustomed to being without its mother for two to three hours a morning while it attends a kindergarten. At first this will probably be for one morning a week and then two mornings a week until the child seems able to cope with more time away from home. During this time a child gradually becomes able to meet more children while away, but with the security of seeing its carer again before too long. However, this will not necessarily happen at all pre-school institutions because some children attend pre-school centres or nursery schools where they are subjected to intellectual 'lesson' content—where they are even taught how to read and write.

As grandparents would, so kindergarten should

In the chapter on education and elsewhere we have explained why and how damage is done to the physical body through an early intellectual education at home and school. We have discussed the importance of pre-school education, which has nothing to do with the acquisition of intellectual concepts but everything to do with learning how to get on with other people. In many ways it is more ideal that a child does not go to kindergarten and imitate the ways of others—their language and their behaviour. A kindergarten is ideal when it is based on learning such as that once acquired from its grandparents in the extended family— household skills such as using, putting away and keeping objects in their own 'home', so to speak, so that there is order in the scheme of things. Such tidiness in practical affairs will assist the ordering of thought processes, so laying the foundations for clear thinking in adult years. Children learn to 'think with their hands', and doing repetitious activities that are allied to household and human tasks in life strengthens their will-power.

Social skills

Holding hands while singing does much for the inner being of a child. It is a discipline that becomes a self-discipline, for a little child learns through such an activity that there are others occupying their own space and need their own space. They learn that there is a time for all things and that time must be allowed for others with differences in learning ability. It is at this time that the foundation for healthy, well-balanced relationships are made. Through a structured, regular routine and rhythm in a morning at kindergarten, children will learn to interact with others through the guidance of the adults in charge of the establishment. The adults should ideally be grandparents, in age if not in reality, for older people usually relate to young children easily. The atmosphere should be calm and free from tension, so that the children feel better within themselves when they experience security and have confidence in those around them. Through imitation they will learn to crayon, paint, help make bread, wash the dishes, sweep the floor and put each object away in its proper place, so that they know where to find it next time, and be fully occupied in child-appropriate activities—not intellectual, 'clever' activities devised by adults and *taught* to the children who are still at the stage of *imitation*. They will learn to appreciate the world around them when the teacher talks with reverence about the stones, the plants and the flowers, and tells the story in a quiet, unemotional way while everyone is listening quietly and attentively. Through these experiences they gain a sense of responsibility and self-discipline, and learn to listen to the conversation of others and how to respond.

Children must be allowed to learn to play as children in order to work as adults. The socialization and educational process is of enormous significance for the manner in which the play of a child is transformed into the work of an adult. Play, as we have argued, is work for a child, and this work ideal should not be destroyed, as it so often is by the longstanding teaching and learning methodologies in mainstream education. So many simply hate school, and the knowledge of this should have been reckoned with long ago. It is beyond belief that academic educationists have not grasped this patent fact; if they have, they have not known what to do about it. We are *not* in any way advocating the once-popular 'play way' strategies, or in some way turning learning into a kind of game, or making it 'fun'.

Caning and other punishments for lazy or inattentive pupils is now a thing of the past, but children are consistently found to loathe and detest schools. The increase in the number of arson attacks on educational establishments is a new and worrying trend.

One of the first things children do, when given the opportunity without adult interference, is to enjoy themselves. They are, in fact and in effect, expressing themselves artistically, in however a simple and rudimentary way, however primitively, and as such are *playing*. Should this fact not serve as a pointer for how educational principles should be influenced? This propensity is very soon 'drowned out' by the increasing adult expectation for children to learn, which has always been present from birth in any case, and the child's willingness to please and co-operate with grown-ups is seized upon and exploited almost to the exclusion of all else. This process entails intellectual methods of imparting information, as these are deemed to be quick and effective. But it must not be forgotten that the whole purpose of education is to *lead* children from being children, whose whole work is play, to adults who do *productive work* for the common weal, for the benefit of others, for the ultimate good of all.

> *Generally speaking, education has followed in the footsteps of our modern civilization which has gradually become more and more materialistic. A sympton of this is the frequent use of mechanical methods in preference to organic methods, and this just during the early years of childhood up to the change of teeth, which is the most impressionable and important time of life. We must not lose sight of the fact that up to the second dentition the child lives by imitation. The serious side of life, with all its demands in daily work, is re-enacted in deep earnestness by the child in its play. The difference between a child's play and an adult's work is that an adult's contribution to society is governed by a sense of purpose and has to fit into outer demands, whereas the child wants to be active simply out of an inborn and natural impulse. Play activity streams outward from within.*

Adult work takes the opposite direction, namely, inwards from the periphery...

But because, through lack of knowledge of the human being, the key to childhood has been lost, all kinds of artificial play activities for children of kindergarten age have been intellectually contrived by adults ... There is no need for the nursery class staff to go from one child to the next to show each one what it has to do. The child does not yet want to follow given instructions. All it wants to do is to copy what the adult is doing.[13]

Rudolf Steiner
The Child's Changing Consciousness

8. Discipline: From Diversion to Negotiation

A teacher (and/or parent) is always an authority for young children and will always be imitated, whether he or she wishes to be or not. But what they take from the adult of an intellectual nature ... works destructively on them. Passing judgements, analysing and evolving theories demand a cutting away from the outside world; they are based on the forces of antipathy, which can be awakened too early in the child. The very necessary feelings of trust and sympathy with its environment will then be destroyed ...

Whenever these forces of antipathy and isolation develop too early, either through extreme demands on the intellect or through an insistence on independent judgement, the result will be a premature rupture of the emotional bonds to other human beings and to nature; this will take place long before the emotional nature is ready and able to stand on its own. They become emotionally stunted and at adolescence will be crippled in their feelings. They will be unable to love anyone or anything with warmth, will find everything boring, and continually will need all kinds of sensations and stimulants from outside in order to arouse their feelings.[1]

Erich Gabert
Educating the Adolescent: Discipline or Freedom

Good habits and discipline

Always bear in mind that you, the mother, are primarily responsible, together with other family members, for instilling good habits by establishing sound domestic routines. Eventually, children *must* learn to do as they are told. This need not be in the manner of strict authoritarianism, establishing some kind of 'punishment and reward' regime, or adopting similar behaviourist methods. However, you should be quite clear that the burden of liability and accountability lies with you, your partner or carer. Close friends and relations are usually reluctant to interfere with the status quo where domestic harmony is involved, except in emergencies and crisis situations.

Good conduct and domestic discipline should date from baby's birth. Mothers do themselves a disservice if they carry baby around until it falls asleep, for as it becomes more conscious it will expect to be put to sleep in this way every time. Eventually, it gets too heavy for this routine, and then the trouble begins. It is not baby's fault that it has not got used to drifting off to a sound sleep in its own cosy bed, and you will be the one to suffer if you give in to temptations like this. A healthy baby will kick and wave its arms, doing its own exercising when not asleep, but the very last thing it needs is being massaged and later exercised energetically with over-stimulating, 'hardening' exercises, which according to childcare 'experts' are advisable in order to promote development and 'fitness'. As ever, it seems, parents actually *want* their children to grow up quickly, and are proud when they do so. But as we have seen, this means encouraging precocity in all manner of ways. This misguided attitude of many mothers to boast that their children are now able to do this or that clever trick is endemic. Whatever else, every mother wants her children to be 'more forward' than those of her neighbour, and to 'do better' than they themselves did. Parents harbour hopes and dreams for their children, all the time attempting to experience, in a vicarious fashion, whatever was lacking in their own childhood.

A changing scene

Avoiding conflict by preventing a battle of wills is wise if you can clearly work out what you want the child to do. You are the loving, kindly authority who leads and guides your child, diverting it to appropriate activities without recourse to physical smacking and hitting, or worse! A child wants to keep moving, and feels physically trapped by inaction, for movement, as an expression of its *will*, is necessary to its overall development. A child likes to see the results of its activities, and this may not please its carers—for many of the actions of a baby, toddler, child and adolescent bring results which range from spilt milk to serious damage to property and person. A baby sitting in a high-chair can have great fun dropping food on the floor, or anything else that is returned to it over and over again. The keywords are *deed* and *endeavour*!

When they are a little older, children love to 'scrub' their crayons round and round or back and forth in order to experience sheer *movement*—it is not just scribble! Children over the age of three love to draw a brush with paint of bright pure red, blue or yellow across a sheet of clean white paper, and see the paint move. So movement, *action* of a disciplined kind in the presence of a calm and collected adult will keep a busy child occupied until it is healthily tired.

Tired and scratchy

When a toddler throws a tantrum, hurling itself kicking and screaming onto the floor, it is probably a result of frustration when trying to make itself understood, but unable to do so because it cannot yet put into words what it wants to say. Usually, 'communication' tantrums will stop once a child can say clearly enough words in order to make itself understood. Never use baby talk to any child, and speak clearly at all times. If clear 'human' speech is not apprehended by children, then abstract thought will not take place later. Tantrums in a shop may be the result of tiredness or nervous exhaustion (in your child, although it will produce the same in you!) for it is easy to forget how tiring it is for a child to go to the shops and be overwhelmed by the size, noise, bustle, and the rows and rows of coloured objects which threaten to fall in on it. It will feel 'scattered', which is the very opposite of what you are striving to achieve—a well-centred child. As you know, it is difficult to make some decisions. So you will understand how much harder it is for an inexperienced child when asked to choose from the overwhelming varieties of sweets and other 'goodies' on offer in the shops. If this unfortunate habit is customary, the bewildered child cannot be blamed if a fit of temper results.

If a child bites someone, instead of retaliating angrily you could say gently, 'Animals bite...' because children don't want to be likened to animals. A strong, healthy child may be very wilful and determined, but this is part of the process of developing a strong will. 'Good', well-behaved children, Rudolf Steiner averred, are those whose spirit cannot properly take hold of their bodies, as these offer too much resistance. On the other hand, so-called 'naughty' or badly behaved children who shout and give a lot of trouble generally, those who are high-spirited and vigorously active, are able to make use of their bodies efficiently. Said Steiner: 'We may even regard the wild screams of the child as most enthralling, simply because we thereby experience the martyrdom the spirit has to endure when it descends into a child-body.'[2] So on the one hand, through *imitation*, a child can be shown how to behave, and on the other hand, discipline can be effected by establishing certain daily rhythms by simple repetition. If the same regular habits are followed—getting up and getting dressed, cleaning teeth and washing, eating what you provide for breakfast, and so on, then you are clearly in charge.

Before a child is about six years old it does not fully realize that many of its actions are *inconsequential*. For instance, until this age it may thoughtlessly and impulsively run across a road with no regard for its dangers. After this age it will gradually learn to take a modicum of responsibility, but still only from a child's viewpoint—which is not that of an adult. So it will need watchful help when necessary. As the child's will develops the adult can choose not to get angry, because a child loves to see an adult get angry—and the will loves power! So if you can remain calm in the face of the growing wilfulness of your child you will not get *too* upset over anything. Laughing at a child, mimicking its words or actions, or ridiculing it should never take place, because it builds distrust during childhood and leads to lack of confidence in adulthood. Excessive, immoderate attention from an adult, and too much intellectual 'reasoning' with them, brings on a kind of nervousness in children. They cannot always understand what is happening, and confusion and anxiety results. Consciously ignore innocuous behaviour; never hold post-mortems, and certainly don't nag them. Adults are able to help guide the childish will along proper ways; *on no account destroy it.*

Working towards independence

In general, discipline is best effected by getting involved with children's activities. Shout only in emergency, be firm and resolute, and avoid the use of 'No!' or 'Don't!' if at all possible, because toddlers are prone to obstinacy, pushing away anyone who opposes their desire for space—and please do not construe this as personal rejection. Replace negative commands with a cheery 'We will do this together...' or something similar. By using 'we' and employing well-chosen words in a firm tone of voice which conveys to the child that you expect to be obeyed, such resolute tactics may be employed instead of negative commands. Don't shrink from exercising your own will-power; strengthen your inner determination when you feel like giving in, when you feel your inner strength fading away. You will probably feel that you are being constantly 'worn down' and lacking in energy and resourcefulness. But all is by no means lost, for it is during this very time that children's sense of fantasy begins to assert itself. Children like to see movement and change, and effect these themselves through manipulation of objects—including human objects—in imaginative ways. Remember that when something new is experienced, children of all ages need space and time to grow accustomed. They find it difficult to adapt to sudden changes, such as when families move away—taking their children with them, of course. Such children 'vanish' in very deed, and this can be upsetting and bewildering to them as well as their friends.

So by disciplining your children lovingly, calmly and thoughtfully, measures taken that are based on knowledge of their spiritual needs as they gradually make themselves at home in a strange world will be seen to be effective. Children need to learn to exercise their imagination through healthy activities at home, on outings with parents to places of interest and so on. You are in charge, so never forget your responsibilities; get involved with your children, for this is what they *need*. Mothers and fathers who 'keep their distance' and nervous parents who are unsure of what they are doing there are in plenty. But you must always have your own well-considered aims and objectives in mind, so make sure that they are met if at all possible. These requirements do not include cosmetics, jewelry and suchlike, however, for children need to grow into the world slowly, and should not be made to feel more 'grown up' than they actually are. Swimming lessons (in harsh, chlorinated water), sports coaching sessions, gymnastics, attending dancing classes—indeed, over-stimulation of all kinds through activities that entail the giving of instructions rather than simple imitation at too early an age—are best avoided.

Taking into consideration your child's age and the activities it can handle, and depending on the season of the year and the weather, supervised 'work' could include helping in the house or garden, finger-knitting and other craft activities, walking in the park, playing outdoors with a bucket of water and/or sand as available. A child who is able to learn and explore through supervised activities is unconsciously rewarded by a continuation of these on the assumption: 'If

I am good, Mum will let me do this again...' Whenever a child is up out of bed, you should, as far as is possible, know what your child 'is up to'. If there's quiet, or silence, quickly ascertain what is going on, for sudden quiet frequently means *trouble.*

No one can reason with a small child

A small child has no moral sense and no logic, so when an adult barks: 'I told you *not* to do that ... ' 'How many times have I told you not to do that ...?' 'What did you do that for ...?' and explains and threatens, the flow of words is like water off a duck's back. A child will shut out the voice which seems to be going on and on, and this is the kind of scenario that starts it off taking no notice of what is said. It has to do so to protect itself from nervous exhaustion! *A small child cannot be reasoned with!* What is worse, and *imitation* being the key to it all, if you end up by shouting then your child will shout back at you. You did it first, and 'we' copy our wonderful, adored mother or father, don't we? So it is always best to *teach your child by doing.* Rehearse over and over again just what you want it to do, taking an active part yourself down to the smallest detail, instead of simply *telling* the child.

Moralizing does not work

Psychologists frequently promote their 'informed' opinions based on the evidence gained by research according to whatever theory happens to be in vogue at the time. Invariably, the arguments put forward are intellectual in approach: 'Tell your child ...' 'Explain to your child ...' Praise your child ...' 'React reasonably when ...' 'Emphasize to your child ...' 'Don't ...' 'Do ...'—and so it goes on! It is our belief that it is no use giving a child continual praise, constant reinforcement (positive or negative) or explanations about why, what and how, or intellectual definitions of rules and suggestions for behaviour modification. Until your child is about seven years of age, what you are as a person, how you behave, how you treat other people and how you operate in the world is what matters to it, although for the most part your attitudes are absorbed unconsciously. After the age of seven children are capable of being disciplined by what is *said to them*. After puberty, assuming the adolescent has had a suitable and appropriate education at home and at school, then he or she can be reasoned with. To attempt to moralize with children before the age of puberty is a waste of time and energy.

Don't tidy up after your child

If you want to make yourself a slave to your child, make sure that you pick up its clothes off the floor, put its toys away and clear up its muddles. Repeat this day after day, and you have succeeded in conditioning it never to do anything for itself—unless it simply has to. Not only will its *will* become weak, but it will develop inappropriate expectations of others as well, and that may lead to conflict in the workplace and in the home. We probably all know someone who is happy to sit back and be waited upon, and who gets annoyed when asked to do something. Discipline need not be harsh or coercive; by cheerfully and consistently setting an example of self-discipline in your own habits, your child will also become disciplined, responsible and self-reliant in later life. If you encourage your child to put away its toys at the end of each day while it is young, helping it to do so, saying, 'We will put away the toys now,' then this will show your child—*by doing*—how to keep order in its surroundings. Actually, it is not even necessary to say those words to a little child, for as you will notice, when you pick up a toy and put it in the basket or box, your child will follow every gesture you make. It will imitate what you are doing right down to the way you approach and accomplish the task, and so conflict is avoided. Remember: what you do, they do. But progress is not instant, because the will is developed by doing the same task time and time again. And most importantly, perhaps—if you tell a child to do something—*make sure that it is done.*

Think carefully before you place too much responsibility on the shoulders of any child. They may not wish to refuse your request, yet at the same time may be unsure of the proper thing to do, and this often leads on to nervousness, uncertainty and lack of confidence. Mia Kellmer Pringle suggests that:

> to thrust too much responsibility onto a child or to do so too early may have harmful effects. Without the neces-sary understanding of what is involved and of the probable consequences of a particular decision or choice, responsibility will be perceived as a burden. He may neverthelesss be prepared to shoulder it but at a high cost in terms of anxiety: or he may refuse to accept it, spending much time and ingenuity in devising ways of avoiding responsibility, perhaps wishing and dream-ing, but rarely doing.[3]

The will wants power

As we have already emphasized, a structure and a rhythm to each day gives your child security; repetition of certain activities strengthens its will; and always bear in mind the necessary responsibility of being a person worthy of imita-tion. These three maxims are absolutely vital. A toddler will challenge its parents as its *will* develops, and that is why parents must be gently firm and decisive about what it is allowed to do; for the will, as manifestation of its developing ego, wants power, demands power, thrives on power. It is *before* a child is two years of age that control must be gained by parents, for if an 18-month-old child punches an adult in the face and gets away with it, then it forms a precedent for patterns of behaviour that may lead to more violence towards others later on. If your toddler punches or 'attacks' a visitor you should act immediately to redress matters. Pick the child up, give it a reassuring kiss and cuddle, and gently but firmly say something like the rhetorical question: 'We don't hit people, do we?' *You* must be alert at all times to such forms of behaviour, and crises and other moments of tension should never be allowed to develop into a scenario where downright appeasement is resorted to. There are many parents who are frightened or even terrified of their young children, and live in constant fear of their older children.

Watch the signs

A child can quickly become over-excited if it is being chased, or over-stimulated in ways mentioned earlier. It cannot pull itself together from out of its own resources in order to calm down and relax, simply because its still incarnating ego is not strong enough. In a manner of speaking, *you* must act as the child's ego on such pressing occasions. An adult must anticipate likely results of any such over-excitement, and choose the right moment to draw an activity to a close by providing a diversion of some kind. If something is to be taken away, put something else in its place. Children and adults who become distraught or even hysterical need to be helped by quiet, calm actions of others who are able to be objective about the whole situation. Never allow your child, whether in your own home or in someone else's, to take liberties such as climbing onto the coffee table and scrambling over the furniture; and *never* be tempted to laugh at such antics, or applaud them. Invitations for visits tend to dry up after an episode or two of such unruliness, and many a close friendship has collapsed after the arrival of children. In the long run, it is your child who will suffer, for no one likes the badly behaved child of inconsiderate and insensitive parents. You are obliged, during these early years, to direct the child's behaviour from your own centre of consciousness, namely, your ego. In the last resort, *you* are responsible.

Rudolf Steiner gives instances of excessively choleric behaviour on the part of parents and teachers frightening and shocking children during their early years; this may result in digestive and other metabolic disorders, and perhaps rheumatism and related diseases in adulthood. Similarly, the moods and actions of a parent, teacher or significant other whose temperament is extraordinarily melancholic may so affect the children that their life of feeling is 'chilled', and such constraints placed upon their inner life could cause irregularities of breathing and blood-circulation, heart trouble and allied complaints to occur in their later life. A phlegmatic teacher whose basic indifference inhibits free exchange of thoughts and feelings with the pupils may induce nervous disorders when they are older. Lack of firm direction and guidance from an excessively sanguine adult may result in children suffering later on from listlessness and lack of vitality and zest for life, as well as lack of will-power and perseverance in face of difficulties.[4]

Every child likes to know where it stands and where the boundaries are, and likes to keep to an everyday routine in order to feel at ease in its own home. It is adults who have problems connected with inner disquiet as a rule, because of the stresses of the many responsibilities they have. Patience and time are necessary for reassuring a child that you are interested in what it is saying. Disinterest in a child may convey a silent message: you are not worth listening to; you have nothing to say; you aren't very lovable, and suchlike. (There are those who are involved with caring for 'battered' women—there are battered men also—who confirm that some men may become violent when they cannot clearly express their feelings and their thoughts, and feel frustrated, inadequate and mortified as a result of not being able to articulate them. Elsewhere we have emphasized that effective communication skills are of paramount importance, for it always takes two to make a conversation—and a 'bargain'.)

Does your child ask questions all day?

Sometimes parents feel inadequate when their child gets to the stage of asking 'Why...?' all day long. The questions are never-ending, and who knows the answers to some of them anyway? For the most part their questions indicate the intense desire of children to initiate conversation and practise the words they know and others they are not sure of, and answers such as adults understand them are *not* required. Such a conversation may be, 'Why are the flowers that colour?' and the answer could be, 'Aren't they pretty?' or 'They are pretty, aren't they?' An answer employing strictly correct scientific terms and reasons is not necessary, or indeed wanted. Another way to deal with the endless questions is to ask, 'What do you think?' and then listen carefully to your child's answer, for much in the way of unconscious wisdom will come from a little child without its being aware of it and usually it cannot repeat what it said if asked to do so. Some children are thwarted by a carer who becomes irritated and impatient and can't be bothered with them. For example, a long time ago a small boy looking out of the bus window was heard to say: 'Why does a cow have four legs, Mummy?' and was answered by both a clip over the ear and, 'Don't ask such silly questions and keep your mouth shut, stupid!' Over 20 years later he is probably still following this 'advice'. We hear endless discussions concerning breakdowns in relationships, and search for the reasons why. The answer often lies in someone's childhood experiences of incidents long since forgotten.

Much that goes on in the depths of the soul, especially so, perhaps, in the case of children, is profoundly significant for later life. Orthodox psychiatrists meet such cases in their daily work, and are of course well aware of this kind of thing. Even events so seemingly insignificant as a child being unjustly accused of some misdeed of which it is entirely innocent:

> ... but it suited the convenience of those around him to throw blame on the child, so as to have an end of the matter. Now children are very specially sensitive to unjust accusation; but as life now is, although such an experience may have bitten deeply into the childish life, the later soul-life put another layer of existence over it, and as far as everyday life is concerned the child forgot it. And indeed it may very well never crop up again. But suppose that in his fifteenth or sixteenth year this boy should experience fresh injustice, perhaps at school; then that which has lain dormant below in the surging waves of his soul begins to stir. The boy need not know that a memory of what he had formerly endured is rising to the surface, he may have different concepts and ideas on the subject. But if his earlier experience had not occurred he might simply have gone home, perhaps grumbled and complained, and shed a few tears, and that would have been the end of the matter.[5]

This could have serious consequences in later life. The same child may well, as an adolescent or adult, suffer a similar injustice. The earlier experience will probably have been long forgotten by child and accuser, but the effects may now be catastrophic, perhaps involving depression and suicide. For, Steiner asserts:

> The first injustice had, however, been experienced, and although, as I make a point of saying, the boy need have no recollection of it, yet it works! It becomes active beneath the surface of the soul-life just as there may be

movements beneath the surface of a calm and glassy sea, and what might have ended in a few grumblings and tears now becomes the suicide of an adolescent![6]

This is the kind of information which every parent and teacher should know, and take seriously into consideration. Mental disorders are becoming more and more widespread, and distressing to those involved. It is significant that many sufferers find themselves unable to give any reason for their depression, inner tension, stress, insomnia or whatever. Many cases of violent behaviour, domestic and otherwise, occur for no apparent or obvious cause.

Imaginative stories

Your child is disciplined by you through your actions, through what is visible or intuited by it. As it grows older a different method of discipline is effective, for a child after the age of seven or so is more influenced by what is said to it. You will be able to use your imagination to make up a story to suit the occasion. It may follow an incident in which a child has punched and hurt another, causing it to cry. Such an aggressor could be told a story of your own invention at a later, quieter moment. It doesn't need to be too complicated, as the following example indicates: 'Once, the mother of a nest of little birds was hit on the wing by a child who threw stones at her, so that she couldn't fly about to get food for her young ones, and couldn't even fly up to the nest to see if they were safe, or keep them warm. She was very worried, and fretted about her chicks, but by the time her wing was better, and she could fly again, her little ones had died of cold and starvation.' Nothing more need be said; the child is then left free to work it out in its imagination. It is always a good thing for you to invent such 'cautionary' stories of your own. Don't be shy of doing so—practice works wonders! But remember: *never* attempt 'explanations'.

No extraneous 'bribes', please

You will by now have noticed that we do not emphasize or encourage giving rewards in the form of 'stars', money or 'points' which are 'earned' by a child as a result of another's expectations. This kind of 'payment by results' amounts to nothing less than behaviourism, and is more suitable for the training of animals than for child education. We have not placed emphasis on punishment or withdrawal of privileges. Repeated banishments to the bedroom eventually engender feelings of rejection and abandonment, leading to the 'nobody wants me' syndrome. Stress should always be placed on the acquisition of self-discipline in adult and child, without recourse to crude deterrents. Through work which needs to be done, rewards are seen in the form of what has been achieved—a tasty meal, a completed craft activity, kind words to another, and so on. It is actually the activity involved, like virtue, that brings its own reward, for repetition brings its own success in that we each can 'do better next time', and that we can see constant improvement in what we make and do. This may seem idealistic, but from another point of view it ensures that later on, as an adult, his or her actions are performed through a conscious, inner impulse or act of will arising from inner freedom and *not* as a result of coercion, when it is a matter of another's will being obeyed. It is positively degrading for us all, as moral beings, to have to rely on outer rules and regulations where ethics is concerned.

It is easy to forget that children are always 'trying things out'—and that includes 'trying' *you*! Everything is new to them, and they are keen to explore, examine, take things apart, see how things work—see how you 'work'—by means of your reactions to their probings. You may get bored with the world, but they don't. You may get tired of being 'tried out', but to them it is a learning experience. They are learning all the time; they never stop, so do your best to see to it

that they are learning what is wholesome and truly beneficial. They have far more time than you have, either to 'play
up' or be occupied in a constructive and wholesome manner. But if you can involve them in 'helping out' in some way
or other so much the better, for then both parties derive
satisfaction and gain from the experience.

Nine or ten—such a sensitive age

Elsewhere we have mentioned the changing awareness of a
child at about nine or ten years of age. It begins to see the
world differently than hitherto; whereas earlier it had felt
the world to be one with itself, and even in some respects as
an extension of itself, now it is more detached and objective
about its environment and those individuals closest to it.
During this phase of its childhood it may ask a question
which bears more behind it than may be immediately apparent. How this is responded to is crucial to its later well-being,
for the answer to its question may affect your child long into
the future, when the incident has been forgotten. At this time
it goes through a mid-childhood 'identity crisis' (just as
there is a mid-life crisis at about 35 years of age in an adult's
life), becoming more critical of its parents, its family, its
home, its school, its teachers, and its friends. Hurtful remarks are often made by a child at this time. Again, certain
things have to be ignored, but explanations are appropriate
for a child of this age, preferably brought to life with
examples of others' reactions to similar incidents—a picture
of others' dilemmas, crises and problems, and how these
were resolved—from real life if possible.

The behaviour and attitudes of a child of this age is
indicative of the fact that the ego is penetrating—incarnating—more effectively, and is striving to establish itself more
firmly. This is why all kinds of doubts concerning its 'presence' in the world crop up. They become interested in *who*
they are, who their parents are, and their ancestry and

relations in general. Their intellectual powers, soon to become firmly established with the approaching milestone of puberty, are strengthening all the time. This means that they feel less sympathetic and hence less 'at one' with their family and general environment, but more antipathetic, and so more objective, more detached, more distant, and hence more critical, analytical and rational. Only now is it appropriate to introduce the element of *reason* into your dealings with your child, and it is a matter of proceeding with great caution and circumspection. Demonstrate to him or her that you—and indeed the whole family—are well and truly supportive, caring and above all interested in a manner that is, well, somewhat more deferential perhaps than previously! That 'foetal ego' must develop and progress!

During this crucial time, when your child is criticizing you and what you say, it will at the same time expect you— as a kindly authority who can be relied on to be consistent and fair—to act as counsellor and guide, and ease the pressures of life. Formerly life was more carefree, but now it begins to feel the pain of experiencing difficulties connected with its own growth as it becomes more clumsy and awkward, which it does at about this time. With the approach of puberty, many children from about the age of eleven or twelve begin to find difficulty in talking to adults and, although wishing to discuss the many questions that occupy them, find the barrier impossible to break through. They suffer more through knowing that another person, perhaps their mother, is wanting to resume the familiar and easy conversations that they once enjoyed together, but her child does not communicate with her. Gabert explains:

> The child feels as though the doors that once were open are now closed; threads that were connected are broken. Very often, the pain will be heightened into defiance, or into a stubborn thrusting away of anything or anyone that comes too near.[7]

Any child feels nervous if an adult cannot make up his or her mind, feeling contempt for a ditherer who can't reach a decision and stick to it. They become frightened if the adults in its life can't cope with their problems—psychological or otherwise. You have to be strong within yourself to cope with your child of ten years of age and older, and this may entail becoming better informed concerning many facets of life that were unrealized before this. It is important to convey the impression to your child that you 'know all the answers' even if you don't—not at the time, anyway! Let children realize that you have had a wide experience of life, and have hidden depths to your character which they do not yet know about. At all costs do not let them lose faith in you, and demonstrate your faith in them.

Anger, frustration and temper tantrums

Parents whose children exhibit severe behavioural problems experience, in common with many other well-meaning parents, feelings of despair, guilt and anguish because they have convinced themselves that they have failed their children. They describe their family life, with its fears and tensions brought about by their insolent and belligerent child's domination and tyranny, as sheer misery. Their unpredictable behaviour towards themselves and others in the family and people in the wider community is frequently the cause of consternation and distress. Parents fear such outbreaks from their child who is 'full of suppressed anger' which erupts unexpectedly and violently towards others in the vicinity. If there are younger siblings they may well imitate the violent behaviour of their older brother or sister, and the parents feel helpless. When questioned, such parents admit that their dear little sons or daughters started to get away with inappropriate behaviour at a very early age, but were not checked. This led on to all sorts of precocious behaviour, a scenario which frequently indicates that encouraging the child to choose for itself probably lies at the root of the trouble. In short, they have most likely been treated as *diminutive adults rather than children*, who were 'cute' and perhaps 'forward'—until they got out of control. Perhaps the initial question to older problem children should be: 'Have you had a carefree childhood, or do you feel that you were deprived of your childhood?' Does anyone ask these children why they feel angry and, if they are asked, are they able to identify or describe their inner problems? It is becoming increasingly evident that many parents are having serious problems with a child or children in the family, even from a very young age.

The kindly authority of parents and teachers for each child between seven and fourteen years is essential. Remember that it is this very factor of authority which helps the child's ego to hold its 'self' together during this stage of the incarnating process. The authority provided by parents and teachers act as a kind of supporting framework or 'scaffold' in this respect. Later, a forceful teenager will test your values and your strength of will again and again, not to mention your patience and stamina. Ultimately, you must have developed yourself and continue to develop yourself so that you are strong enough to stand up for what you value, for the many vicissitudes of life may sap your strength, and even your health. We progress through pain and suffering, and all of us find this out to be true. Clever we may be during our youth and early adulthood, but in so very many respects life does indeed begin at 40, and it is only after that age that we may become truly *wise*.

Stand firm in the face of argument

Discipline for teenagers is a difficult area of discussion. By this time your child will have certain values instilled into him or her directly because of your influence, and that of significant others. Now is the time for intellectual discourse on the whys and wherefores of a situation, or a cause and its effect(s). You may put your viewpoint forward and it may seem to be ignored, but even if not outwardly acknowledged it will be taken in and thought about. Now is the time to be adaptable but strong-willed yourself. The framework of authority referred to just now will be kicked away by the young adolescent as the ego incarnates more and more deeply. Your teenager needs a certain flexibility of approach, and a certain freedom, but for his or her own well-being certain rules should be enforced, perhaps in co-operation with the parents of your child's friends. If you all stick together on certain issues, then you may survive the onslaughts upon your equilibrium more calmly.

Remember that peer pressures are at their strongest during adolescence, and your children are quite capable of betraying you before they do their cronies. This kind of behaviour is hard to take, but don't hesitate to phone up other parents to ascertain where the party is, who is going to be present, and when it is due to finish. Show them that parents can stick together too! You will have to work out your approach to alcohol, drugs, borrowing the car and many other hazards to adolescent well-being. We quote Gabert again:

> Every teenager becomes unpleasant at times, even impossible! Often they will break through the wall that sets them apart and will attach themselves passionately to another person as they once used to do, but they know that this is only a temporary thing, and the essence of their childhood can never return. The agonizing detachment is truly final. And the young person has no way of knowing why he or she struggles to stay apart, and struggles to prevent anything from disturbing their solitude.
> They cannot bear that others probe their feelings,

even though in younger years it never mattered. Now they know that they would hate to show their feelings and desires to any other person, even though they often feel driven to reveal them ... A particular element of this inner life is the feeling that it is closed away in itself, so that anyone who tries to peer in must be repulsed.[8]

As we have explained elsewhere, it is at this time that the birth of the astral body takes place. If this 'birth' is hastened, brought into being prematurely as a result of premature experiences natural to adult life, then permanent damage is done to the soul and spirit of the individual. The world is now seen in a new light, and events can be seen with a clearer vision than before. Before puberty children are able to *feel* the world, but after puberty, because of their detachment from the world, they *perceive* it.

Don't be bullied by your child or your child's friends. You must stand firm, even if you are sworn at, and later your reward will be your child's respect for your doing so. If you listen beyond the spoken words you may realize that your brash and confident teenager is actually nervous of being involved in certain situations, and is hoping that you will help out by refusing to allow him or her to go to a certain party or 'rave', or into a situation which is unknown or feared. They need to be able to tell their friends that their mean, bossy mother or miserable 'old man', who are both 'past it' anyway, won't let them go out—but actually they may well be relieved to have a scapegoat or excuse. Remember the enormous pressures that children are under these days. You were your child's model in its early years, and still are, and you carry this responsibility whether you like it or not. You can follow your children only as far as the door, so it may be largely a matter of taking the line: you can always pray for them!

Constant throughout this book is the understanding and hope that by means of communication, discussion and negotiation you will present a united front when bringing up and 'disciplining' a child, or children. A house divided against itself will fall, and a child will divide one parent from another at times if it can, so do not allow one to be played off against the other. Be firm after you have determined your course of action out of hearing of the child, and follow a consistent approach in all matters. A self-disciplined adult can discipline a child, not by threats and physical violence but through example, firmness and—later on—by negotiation and maintaining communication. In discussion with a very dear friend with 40 years' teaching experience, she said:

> I feel very sorry for children and parents in this day and age. In my simple country childhood—and yours—the rules were there, there were far fewer temptations, and perhaps 'if in doubt, hug'. That is, if you're not quite sure how, or if, blameworthy or guilty your child is, hug first—often this clarifies the situation without needing recriminations if you have prejudged, and judged wrongly. Otherwise, as no doubt you already know, you just play along, day by day, doing your best and hoping for the best!

Certainly, communication helps—and hugging is a great idea! It is not always realized that it strengthens the ego. Pressure of any kind on the body always stimulates the ego of both parties—in this case the hugger and the hugged, and this is always a good thing. Pressures exerted in our earliest weeks and months of life are invariably of the kind that evokes confidence and trust, not to mention affection. Later in life we assert and accept pressures of various kinds—by kissing, the shaking (and squeezing) of hands, the arm around the shoulder, the taking by the elbow, and so on. But the hug, which dates back to babyhood, is the signal of ego greeting ego *par excellence*. So carry on hugging!

Punishment or reward

Carefully thought out 'disciplinary measures' have been devised by psychologists according to the particular philosophy they approve of. The practice of 'behaviour modification' is popular among educators, and is an attempt to modify a child's deviant behaviour. A record is kept by the child of its 'progress' according to how it has behaved throughout the day. This method of encouraging self-discipline is a brave attempt to bring the child's behaviour to its consciousness, so that it learns to recognize what is inappropriate and what is acceptable. However, this approach is fundamentally feeble and artificial. There is no substitute for tackling *every* problem squarely and fully, otherwise 'unfinished business' may come back to haunt you. Once the acceptable behaviours are identified, they are reinforced with 'pleasurable outcomes' and removed from enjoyable activities if the behaviour has been unacceptable. All those involved with the child agree to certain conditions and procedures, and parents, teachers and peer groups are encouraged to treat the child in the same manner. A points system is devised to mark the chart, and the child agrees to follow certain guidelines in his or her 'contract'. But pause to consider: this is precisely how animals are trained—and we are not animals.

This kind of intellectual exercise is very time-consuming, and is quite ineffective for younger children. In the case of an older child, the initial response may be favourable, but it gradually decreases in effectiveness. The most rewarding part of it *from the child's point of view* is that it is continually under surveillance, and is thus getting attention from just about everyone in its life—great! The 'best' of it from an adult's point of view is that something is being seen to be done, and done tidily: contract, record, signed record or form, and reward or withdrawal of privileges. If such a system is started with a child at an early age, it will be conditioned to such a method of control, and become more and more experienced in the art of deception and manipulation of systems. By the time it is a teenager, little will be accomplished through this method of 'control' *unless the child wishes it to work*, and chooses of its own free will to take control of its own behaviour—without external and extraneous rewards. Ultimately, a child must become 'moral' through its own efforts. Talking alone is rarely effective, as is any kind of 'preaching'. Morality can be induced by implementing educational methodologies over a child's school years when these are based on a thorough knowledge of the whole human being.[9]

Most parents do their best

Various authorities have said that such and such a method must be followed in bringing up a healthy child, and various disciplines were accepted by paediatricians in the past which took no account of the individual circumstances of baby and parents. Some decades ago, Dr Truby King advocated that a baby should be fed once every four hours, and this practice, when adopted, plunged both mother and baby into a state of nervous tension. Mothers of children born in the 1950s and 1960s say that their children's upbringing was a matter of 'trial and error', that they now feel guilty about the way they obeyed such dictums, and wish they had felt more free to cuddle and hug their children. They said that they could have loved them more. Babies, they were told, had to learn how to behave. Mothers later claimed that they were 'dehumanized' by this approach, and so were their children.

Then came the doctors who encouraged 'responding to baby's needs' and urged that the child be diverted rather than hit or smacked. Others also had an allegedly child-centred approach, and parents felt that they had been given permission to feel comfortable with their baby. During the sixties and seventies fathers were encouraged to take an interest in all aspects of the pregnancy and assist with the baby's care after the birth, and nowadays it is almost the norm for fathers to be present at the delivery if permitted by the medical team. Indeed, European Union legislation provides for fathers to take unpaid paternity leave for periods of up to three years!

Baby-rearing is now big business

As a result of psychological research babies and parenting became big business, and it was then, we suggest, that the trouble really started for parents. The so-called child-centred approach meant to some people that the child should be brought up realizing its own potential; it could and should decide everything for itself. Many misconceptions arose concerning this approach. Parents are told by psychologists that by the age of two or three a child begins to have some moral sense and is able to make some elementary decisions about minor moral issues.[10] This is the sheerest nonsense. Responding to baby's needs became responding to baby's demands in all things, adopting a kind of 'baby and child know best' philosophy. In addition, pressures on parents escalated as the future became, and still is, grim as far as obtaining work and keeping it. Gilbert Childs well remembers the derisive laughter of his students when he told them 30 years ago that by the end of the century it would be a privilege to have a job; getting employment in some capacity would become increasingly difficult, and that they would be glad to work for nothing.

As a result of pressures on parents and their expectations of their children's development, big business in baby and child education equipment and texts boomed. Parents are bombarded by psychologists as well as commercial interests, who urge them to teach their child by various methodologies, to encourage it in its acquisition of concepts, to educate it even while in the uterus, and encourage and stimulate, stimulate and encourage it—to be *precocious.* Children who are encouraged by parents and teachers to believe that they have the right to decide for themselves when they are very young will later on, as mature persons, become dependent on authority when they should be free and capable of making their own decisions and stand on their own feet rather than be dependent on advice, counselling and exhortation from others. Mothers and fathers feel under great pressure to do things perfectly, but perfection comes in many forms, so it seems that it is a matter of choosing the right programme! Parents say how confusing it is when the advice so readily available in so many hundreds of books on children is so conflicting and contradictory. They may feel failures if their child does not meet everyone's expectations. The difficulty was and still is that the *needs* of the infant, child and adolescent are not yet fully comprehended because a true knowledge and recognition of our spiritual origins is not yet sufficiently widespread. The main purpose of this book is to draw attention to these needs.

> *If the young child has been cheated out of a close, loving relationship to his or her surroundings, the forces of antipathy in puberty will be far too strong. Their rightful task is to push back what is outside in order to create in the teenager the inner soul-space from which he or she can forge—with growing independence—their* own *connections with the world. But if this pushing back, because it is premature, proceeds too violently, the separation from other people will be absolute; and an impenetrable wall will be erected. The young person will not be able to reach out to others ... The desire for power, which often appears in these troubled years, is due to this combination of excessive antipathy with the hunger to become conscious of self. In a crippled emotional life, the ego is experienced by the exertion of power over other people.*[11]
>
> Erich Gabert
> *Educating the Adolescent: Discipline or Freedom?*

9. Technology—A Mixed Blessing?

Dr Steiner's message was that the ordinary persons in the street were greater than we knew, and that 'it doth not yet appear what they shall be'. We were told that the methods of production of the necessaries of life would soon be entirely revolutionized, that even work would be taken out of the hands of human beings, and all the world would be supplied by a few skilled engineers. What, then, would be the destiny of the poor? 'Man is not on this planet to be the slave of his brother,' declared Margaret MacMillan, 'and his brother is not on this planet to enslave him.'

Ilkley Free Press and Gazette
10–17 August 1923

We cannot put the clock back

Your reincarnating child descends from a heavenly world into an earthly world where chaos and noise now seem to rule, despite the efforts of well-intentioned parents to provide a safe, peaceful environment for it. You must never forget that its pre-natal life in the spiritual world was one in which *moral order* reigns supreme. The shock baby experiences on finding itself within the confines of a physical organism is very great, and this cannot be emphasized too much. Everything is new and unfamiliar, and the adjustment process will take up at least the first 21 years of his or her life. We know that it not easy to protect your baby from the effects of modern life and in particular those technological marvels which even adults have difficulty coming to terms with. Of course we cannot put the clock back, and it is our task to face up to it and its influences, whether manifest or hidden, for better or worse. Most technological research and development is aimed at improving efficiency in industry and commerce: its sphere of operations is well and truly within the *economic* sphere, in which the profit motive is paramount. Our social lives have been changed for ever, and the impact of television, biotechnology and communications technology in general is only one example. Beneficial effects there undoubtedly are, but there is always a price to pay, and we are paying very dear in terms of social health and welfare.

A very significant factor which is having devastating effects on social life is that of *fear*. The sources of fear are many and diverse, ranging from the ever-increasing incidence of crime and violence to the sheer rapidity of change, political, economic and social. Some idea of the confusion that a small child feels can be gauged by people's reactions to circumstances with which they are not familiar, such as visiting another country where one's own language is not spoken, and being faced with electronic and other gadgetry with which they are not accustomed. Such situations give rise to fear and tension, and this we do our best to control. The need to understand what is going on around us is rooted deep in human nature; we must make sense of it, otherwise we run the risk of losing touch with reality—yet another consequence of fear. So spare a thought for children; they have a more difficult task than the older generations had, when life was slower, simpler—and safer.

The 'flushing toilet syndrome'

Of course, they will be growing into a world that is new to them and they will adapt and settle in, for they have no choice in the matter. Those of us who are already established in it find it harder to adjust to the inevitably changing circumstances. One of us remembers the first frightening experience in our relatively machine-free childhood—that of flushing the toilet: 'Shall I be sucked down into the unknown by that rushing, gurgling water and disappear for ever?' The other of us remembers his first visit to a relative's house where the toilet was not 'down the garden' and without a flush but in an outhouse 'across the yard', equipped with a porcelain toilet with overhead cistern and long chain complete with handle dangling from it. He hardly knew what it was for, but upon being instructed to pull the chain did so. To his amazement and horror it clanged and banged, snarled and hissed, and down came a torrent of water which he was quite convinced would envelope him and suck him under. We lived on opposite sides of the world, but had similar fears!

Television is no substitute for mum or dad

Every child needs constant reassurance and encouragement from its parents. This need for consolation is on account of the 'fear factor' already mentioned, and it is all too often the case that babies are placed in front of the television set for comfort. The constantly flickering coloured screen may be no more than a kind of diversion, but if a child spends up to 40 or more hours a week bound by television it cannot be active and mobile as it longs to be. However, the TV set is undoubtedly a part of most babies' environment, and the incomprehensible, bewildering, often frightening television 'shots' can affect their inner organs, and even their blood circulation. Their eyes, *necessarily in fixed focus,* are not being exercised efficiently while watching passively the flashing, often garish, *two-dimensional* screen. Children watching television can become completely passive, conditioned not to take an active and lively interest in the *real* world around them; conversation skills are not acquired and an inner loneliness sets in, later to be exacerbated progressively during every stage of their lives.

Arguments against television

A child must be able to relate to other human beings who love it, and it has an actual *need* for such affection. A television set may portray human features and human forms but is a mere machine, which cannot make relevant responses to the feelings and thoughts of its viewing audience. A television is a 'pleasant' means of whiling away one's present life. It could be said, and has been at great length by Jerry Mander in his book *Four Arguments for the Elimination of Television*, that television is a 'totally horrible technology' and that we would be much better off without it. Mander says:

> ... television produces such a diverse collection of dangerous effects—mental, physiological, ecological, economic, political ... that it seems to me only logical to propose that it should never have been introduced, or once introduced, not be permitted to continue.[1]

Television addiction is a very effective way to become deadened to what is going on in the world, and in our interaction with other human beings and with nature. Of course there is not space enough in this book to go into every argument to back previous statements, but several aspects can be mentioned. There is evidence that far from being a medium to inform and stimulate thinking in the viewers, it actually dulls people's awareness. People are presented with such a number of complex issues so quickly that they cannot remember what has been said unless perhaps it is repeated as a phrase *ad nauseam*—a simple political message perhaps. What is transmitted by television has in any case necessarily been *pre-selected*; whatever has been collected is processed, edited, re-edited, revised, represented and invariably detached from its source in place and time. The endless replays, trailers, advertisements and snippets of this and that constitute the surest means possible for creating mental confusion. And all this through a machine which shoots 300,000 red, blue and green phosphorescent dots of light of high voltage 'directly into human eyes and from there to the endocrine system'.[2]

The alien in our home

Television is alienating individuals from each other. The claim that 'we watch television as a family' is not valid because although everyone may be sitting in the room watching television at the same time, each one is alone. People are increasingly suffering loneliness and television; it

> encourages separation: people from community, people from each other, people from themselves ... It creates a surrogate community: itself. It becomes everyone's intimate advisor, teacher and guide to appropriate behaviour and awareness.
>
> Thereby, it becomes its own feedback system, furthering its own growth and accelerating the transformation of everything and everyone into artificial form. This enables a handful of people to obtain a unique degree of power.[3]

When the announcer or weather forecaster gives the time of the next bulletin, the words 'See you then' or 'See you later' or similar is generally not recognized as the *untruth* that it is. There is of course no direct contact between them and the viewer, but it gives viewers the feeling of familiarity with the TV personality, which is sheer nonsense—they are total strangers.

People seem to be unable to make distinctions between information through a machine and what they could experience directly; for example, at a concert or play. On one occasion a theatrical group was performing in front of a noisy audience who seemed oblivious of what was being acted out in front of them. Eventually, the performance was stopped while one of the actors explained that they were actually performing 'live' and that they were human beings with something to say, and would the audience kindly listen, or leave. This inability to distinguish what is 'real' and what is contrived, artificial, pre-selected, lifeless and unresponsive has resulted in a loss of confidence as people forfeit their own powers of observation. Now they have come to rely on 'scientific research' and empirical data presented also in rapid, piecemeal fashion, edited and moulded according to what these 'experts' want viewers or listeners to receive. The interviewer's personality intrudes to the point of excluding others who are participating; getting as much squeezed into interviews in the time available rather than allowing time for thoughtful responses has become the norm, and so much of what is said passes through the ears. The radio interviewer's favourite utterance is, 'Very briefly, could you say what ... '

Television hinders proper child development

So what is this to do with children? So far we have described a machine which dominates the room, which presents selected facts to the viewer in a form which affects people's physical health and mental and social well-being. It thrusts upon us the viewpoints and values of those who would never actually be 'entertained' in our own home, in person. It gives information that causes fear, misunderstanding, confusion, diffidence and dullness in adults; so what is it doing to less hardened and more vulnerable, developing, impressionable children who are continually being exposed to the sight of adults being ridiculed, parents and teachers being made fools of and treated with contempt by scriptwriters and actors who are not producing comedy and certainly not wisdom as entertainment?

Apart from the danger to their physical health—passive

posture, inactive eye muscles, the concentrated passage of energy from the television to the viewer and the flicker effect with the risk of television epilepsy—there are other dangers, to children and adults. Children, inert and non-resistant while watching television, erupt when their inner tension is released, when they stop watching the screen. There is mounting evidence that this outer passivity, overcoming a healthy child's natural desire for continual movement through running, jumping, hopping, climbing and exploring the immediate environment, conceals an inner, purposeless 'activity'. This is stopped and then started again, oscillating back and forth between those two poles of action and repression, and is a

> major cause of hyperactivity; fast movement without purpose...which comes bursting outward in aimless random, speedy activity...They are quiet while watching. Then afterwards they become overactive, irritable and frustrated...I believe that in extreme cases the frustration inherent in the TV experience can lead to violent activity, whatever the content of the program. Artificially teased senses require resolution. It is bizarre and frightening, therefore, that many parents use television as a means of calming hyperactive children.[4]

To engage in a *purely intellectual* 'conversation' between adults and young children by means of questions, explanations and suggestions can be a waste of time because children cannot grasp abstractions. Young children do not know the difference between what is real and what is make-believe. Some years ago in Mexico a number of child deaths were reported: children were reported to be throwing themselves off the roof of a building in order to fly like 'Mighty Mouse'. How is it that when a character in a 'soap opera' is obliged to 'die' as part of the plot *adults*, in their thousands, send in floral tributes to the television studio concerned, and letters of condolence? Even a *live* interview is set up prior to the time it is shown. Many items amount to outright deceit. Sometimes shots of people are shown wearing summer clothes, the landscape indicating that it is indeed summer, but the interview is taking place with a reporter who is in a country that is experiencing winter, as is the audience at home. 'Library pictures' appear day after day, even week after week, all giving the illusion that they represent 'live' news coverage. Illusions are *lies*, and of all the media, television must surely be the Beelezebub.

Television is a lie to our organism

The 'pictures' on television are not real. They are a series of 'static' images put out in rapid sequence so that when they are shown on screen they appear to be moving and so 'alive'. In this manner they manifest themselves as a double lie to our organism—and that includes our perception and understanding. They can be speeded up or slowed down or altered in all sorts of ways. Therefore what is a series of untruths, distortions and unreal situations is being presented in programmes and advertisements. Now evidence is being collated to prove that children, and indeed adults, cannot distinguish what is 'hard news' and what is made up. Many people are quite out of touch with certain realities: where milk comes from, how apples grow, what fresh, unprocessed vegetables look like, and so on. Worst of all, perhaps, they cannot tell the difference between the real blood coming out of real but dead or wounded human beings, or animals, and actors smeared with tomato ketchup, or the 'bloodless', squashed animated-cartoon characters that are miraculously restored to life again and again—and all without a single cry of pain!

Much of the violence is being absorbed and internalized via the cartoons on television, film and video. These 'funny' antics are now being introduced to adult audiences in the guise of short bursts of entertainment to fill a two or three minute slot in the programme. One grotesque, semi-human character was seen strangling another misshapen, strangely coloured semi-human character, and the camera focused for a few seconds on the increasing redness of the veins starting out from the eyes and their sockets while the aggressor snarled, 'I like being angry!' What can possibly be the purpose of such a tasteless representation of humanity's sheer wickedness and inhumanity? The audience might possibly laugh at such antics, but the many victims of such assaults in real life and their grieving relatives are certainly not amused.

Everyone experiences anger and frustration at some time in their lives, and this can, and often does, result in violence, 'road rage', cruelty, theft, deception and so on. There are many, many instances shown on television where a person is 'in the way' and eliminated. We have got to the point in our society where if someone chooses to be irritated by something or another person or persons they imagine they have the right to smash, get rid of, 'waste', 'take out', 'eliminate', 'blow away' such sources of irritation—all euphemisms for killing human beings such as we ourselves are. In some homes, if the baby cries it is beaten up—and many die from such a beating. The 'peaceful' way of getting rid of someone who is in the way, a nuisance, is clearly to be seen through the media also.

Notice how the press and television announcers pursue the issue of someone being 'removed from office', or being 'forced to resign from office' in order to make way for another. Sports commentators habitually employ aggressive language heavily laced with military expressions—just watch out for them! The very language of the radio and television announcers is full of warlike terms and words—everything, where possible, is turned into conflict or an uncompromising situation, difficult to turn away from or renegotiate. The questions that interviewers ask are 'closed' rather than 'open' most of the time. Examples of this are sentences which begin with words which presuppose that the one being interviewed will agree or be browbeaten into agreeing with the interviewer's point of view: 'Don't you think that ...', 'Wouldn't it be a good idea if ... ', 'You must agree that...', and so forth. Television is a very persuasive medium for brainwashing its viewers. Examples of 'open' questions are those which begin with 'how' or 'what' or 'why' and these allow the one under cross-examination to think for himself/herself, and questions from interviewers on television rarely begin with how, what or why. Accusations, loaded questions, prejudiced statements, personality worship—all these form the basic stuff of TV.

Created zombies

The trouble with all the hustling that has now achieved perfection among TV 'anchor-persons' is, of course, that the little time needed for reflection before the answer is given during a live broadcast is denied them. It does not take much imagination to know who the king-pin is. The unstoppable, rapid stream of images with images superimposed over other images while someone is talking over a background of monotonous regular droning 'music' or clicking, clacking beats will, we believe, hasten the metamorphosis of thinking human beings into unthinking, accepting, passive, acquiescent albeit frustrated and angry individuals, who are primed to 'blow their tops' when something unforeseen triggers them off!

In addition, 'talking' toys with their muffled, blurred, indistinct messages are depriving children of the opportunity to gain clear, logical speech, and thus the right to be fully human. One in five children in Britain has impaired speech. Speech therapists have expressed their concern about children being given such 'toys', and the results of this created handicap for such a large percentage of children will be far-reaching for many years to come. These children are neither able to listen to adults and follow instructions nor to converse with their classmates. Hence they require follow-up therapy from speech therapists long after they have started attending school. However, the problem may be compounded at school when these children are again exposed to such dehumanizing machines and contrivances as computers. And all this while they are still infants, imitating and imbibing 'dead speech', which instructs them what to do, rather than hearing the warm and reassuring tones of their teacher's voice.

As we have discussed elsewhere, children are 'born' imitators, absorbing what they see and feel around them right into their very being. They imprint these images and feelings into their physical body. It may sound strange but this is evident in the way they walk, talk and gesticulate; these characteristics are observable, and so is their behaviour. We remember the day we carefully watched two little brothers who were looking at books, and when the elder turned a page of his book the younger boy immediately turned a page of the book he was holding; he also copied the facial expressions that indicated inner feelings of interest, amusement, puzzlement and other outer expressions of the inner life of his brother. It was quite clear to us that each action and gesture of the older boy was imitated by the younger child as he sat beside his brother on the sofa. Not a word was said as they 'read' their books.

More insidious effects of television

There are increasing numbers of people, adults as well as children, who are doing actions which they cannot explain or justify when questioned about them later.[5] Children and adults who commit murder, when asked why they did such a thing, reply that they 'just felt like it' or that they 'didn't know why' they acted as they did. They say that they do not know right from wrong, and seem not to have a conscience. The most probable answer to the enormous increase in the incidence of violence to persons and property lies in the likelihood that such people have actually been conditioned to act as they do by having been imprinted by hundreds, per-haps thousands, of murders and acts of violence whilst being 'baby-sat' by a television set. The never-ending stream of 'whodunnits', Western-type films, 'cops-and-robbers' and other 'entertaining' programmes sow seeds of violence in a very real way. 'Copy-cat' crimes are increasing as the news bulletins portray or even recreate the very scene of the mass-murderer shooting at people, or running them down, or whatever. Many of those who commit horrendous crimes are reported to be quiet, withdrawn individuals, and those who know them can hardly connect the person with the deed.

Those people who can remember their childhood days free from television are generally able to describe their outdoor experiences with enthusiasm. They too will remember childhood moments when 'the mere sight of the sky or grass or trees would send waves of pleasure' through them.[6] Television effectively reduces such experiences for impressionable children, and so far mention has not been made of the effects of television on a child's imagination. There are definite limits to the desirability or indeed enjoyment of such vicarious experiences via television.

Insomnia

Psychiatrists and others in the counselling and medical professions report that there are increasing numbers of people suffering from an inability to sleep. There are people who may get as little as one hour's sleep a night. They complain about the constant stream of images going through their mind, churning on, and no matter how they will themselves to clear their mind the activity continues. Their lives are a misery because of this problem. Television fills the mind with images and this leads to 'perceptive exhaustion' due to the constant stream of impressions and images we may not want ever to think about or visualize ever again, but there they remain, and the result of all of this is *fear*! There is an increasing problem with children becoming fearful, experiencing 'night-terrors' which prevent them getting off to sleep. They are awoken by nightmares, and incarnate in an unhappy, weary state of irritability.

One of the most unfortunate effects of television is that its images are taken within the body and retained there. During the night the body re-creates these images and in effect we relive what we have viewed during waking hours. We receive into our 'unconscious' what is projected into us, and the images become part of us: the violent, grotesque, the garish; the poor speech, the materialistic ideas, and so on, all incorporated into our very being. The horror of television, said Dr Erik Peper, 'is that the information goes in, but we don't react to it. It goes right into our memory pool and perhaps we react to it later but we don't know what we're reacting to. When you watch television you are training yourself not to react and so later on, you're doing things without knowing why you're doing them or where they came from.[7]

Television as teacher?

Many of the so-called educational programmes for children are loud, brash, untrue, fast-moving, fragmented and over-brightly coloured. The dialogue is frequently unclear due to poor speech articulation, and dubbed sounds override the character's voice. It is monstrous to present weird creatures as educators of children. A programme devised for television in order to educate the deprived children of America has been popular for many years, and has been imitated in productions elsewhere. Advertising techniques are used to capture and hold the attention of children and adults. Fast-flowing sequences of individual letters of the alphabet are accompanied by a constant patter and chant of sometimes incomprehensible dialogue. The scattered presentation of 'facts and concepts' in this programme will ensure a continuity of scattered, de-centred children. Worst of all, many of the characters' gestures are aggressive and domineering. Invariably, vested commercial interests are behind the production of such programmes; they make money for advertisers, production teams, actors—and others. Many parents believe that such a programme does no harm to their child, and may be beneficial in that it may speed up the acquisition of concepts.

Psychologists with a more limited view of the spiritual nature of human beings are sincerely and enthusiastically promoting communication techniques they have devised for parents to use in order for them to talk more effectively to their children. When we read advice to parents such as the following, we wonder who or what is in charge of whom:

> Praise your child when he is being well-behaved. Give him a cuddle, or a pat on the head, or whatever, when he is watching television quietly. Of course your child may push you away because at that point he would rather watch what is happening on the screen ...[8]

Woolfson claims that there have been many research studies into the problem of children watching television programmes for adults, and that 'there is not one that shows any link between a child's level of aggression and the number of violent television programmes watched.'[9] It seems to us that he is talking nonsense, and the relevant arguments are set out in the chapter on discipline and elsewhere with regard to imitation. This has nothing to do with mere 'modelling', which strictly speaking belongs to the years of adolescence.[10] We have stated again and again that during the early years of a child's life imprinting occurs right down into the vascular system, and may be regarded as 'irreversible conditioning'. That this is not immediately evident to some psychologists is not a valid reason for claiming there is no link between 'a child's level of aggression and the number of violent television programmes watched' for, as we have indicated, it may manifest itself 30 or 40 years later as illness, anti-social behaviour, or even crime. Woolfson claims that:

> One explanation for this lack of connection is 'the dilution factor'—no matter how aggressive or violent one particular television programme might be, its possible influence on the young mind is diluted by the effects of the many non-violent programmes the child also watches... Television literacy—the ability to evaluate critically what is shown on television—can be taught to young children. Talking to your child about the violence he watches on the screen will have an effect on his appreciation and understanding of it. Spend some time with the child, explaining to him that television is not real, and that he should not imitate what he sees on television because it is only make believe.[11]

If Woolfson is correct, how is it that so many adults cannot now discriminate between what is real and what is unreal in what is presented to them on television? Mander stated that this is indeed what is happening, as revealed by research.[12] If this dilution factor argument is valid, why do advertisers continue to 'waste' their money and time? If so, the names and features of their products must be diluted by the number of advertisements and their similarity, which is obviously not the case. This argument in favour of the dilution factor effectively proves that so-called education programmes shown on television or video to children at school are not worth broadcasting because the science concepts would get diluted by the concepts presented in other programmes on other subjects. What muddled thinking! Indeed, the opposite could apply: the number of so-called suitable programmes could be diluted by the number of violent programmes and advertisements.

Computers are compulsive

We seem to be going against current popular opinion by saying that computers are also quite inappropriate for young children in the educational or indeed any other sense. In maturational terms, the appropriate time to learn how to operate a computer is during adolescence and afterwards. Ignorance of how machines work induces nervousness in children and grown-ups alike, as mentioned earlier. Horst Adler quotes Erik Sandberg-Diment:

> Personal computing seems to promise simplicity and deliver complexity. Hardware is not compatible with other hardware, or, when it is, requires a mechanical genius to connect the pieces. Manuals are incomprehensible. Software is an almost endless source of frustration. Confronted with such intricacies, the computer neophyte may feel that either someone has pulled the wool over his eyes or the rest of the world is a lot smarter than it appears.[13]

One thing we are convinced of is that a child must be literate, and able to understand the complexities of language, before it is 'side-tracked' into coping with the mechanics of computing, understanding how to interpret any information given by advertisers about their computers, and how these will help them to process data before they begin to master the difficulties of computer software and its hardware. For example: 'Encrypt scrambles files using a proprietary encryption algorithm. The exact action of this very complex bit-level data scrambling algorithm is determined by the password you specify with the encrypt command.' The time for deciphering this kind of gobbledygook is, we insist, not before puberty!

Video 'games' are anything but

If you want your child to be ruined before it reaches its potential, then buy it plenty of video games and allow it plenty of carefree time to play them. Of course it will become very adept at moving its fingers quickly and with near-perfect co-ordination, but much more will be happening within the inner world of your precious child.

> The loud whizzes, crashes, and whirrs of the video game machine 'blow the mind' and create an excitement that is quite apart from the excitement generated simply by trying to win a game. A traditional childhood game such as marbles, on the other hand, has little built-in stimulation; the excitement of playing is generated entirely by the players' own actions. And while the pace of a game of marbles is close to the child's natural physiological rhythms, the frenzied activities of video games serve to 'rev up' the child in an artificial way, almost in the way a stimulant or an amphetamine might. Meanwhile, the perceptual impact of the video game is similar to that of watching television—the action, after all, takes place on a television screen—causing the eyes to de-focus slightly and creating a certain alteration in the child's natural state of consciousness.[14]

Some 75 years ago, Rudolf Steiner had this to say:

> ... since the middle of the fifteenth century, a gradual transformation of intelligence is taking place. Although it is still very much like that of the Greeks it is undergoing a transformation, and we are in the beginning of it. In the coming centuries and millennia this intelligence will become something very, very different. Even today, it shows a tendency toward what will come in future, a tendency merely to grasp what is

error, untruth, deception; a tendency to ponder only
what is evil ...[15]

We already have computers which possess a kind of
'artificial intelligence', which can 'talk' to one another, and
can 'think' more logically and more swiftly than the human
brain. So we have 'intelligent' machines, more astute and
cleverer than any human being. However, human beings
possess a spiritual nature, a *moral* nature, which operates
according to moral laws. Machines cannot have morals and
do not exist in societies. Modern materialistic science renders
our apprehension of human beings more mechanistic every
day. The earth can survive without machines but cannot
survive without human beings.

*An understanding of the changes in child rearing brought
about the availability of television as a sedative for active and
troublesome preschoolers, changes that lead to poorer
socialization of children, may cause parents to decide that
their difficulties as parents are ultimately increased, not
alleviated, as a result of their use of television as a source of
relief. And finally, a consideration of the inroads television
makes into family life, its effects on meals, conversations,
games, rituals, may persuade parents that the price of accepting television as a force in the family is too high a price to pay.*

*For although we may be powerless in the face of the abstract
machine that modern society has become, we can still assert
our wills in the face of that real and tangible machine in our
homes, the television set. We can learn to control it so that it
does not control us.*[16]

Marie Winn
The Plug-in Drug

10. Courage and Fear

> *Courage: a mental or moral strength to confront and with-*
> *stand danger, fear, or difficulty.*
>
> Longman: *Dictionary of the English Language*

Courage: what is it?

The dictionary will give you all kinds of verbal definitions of courage, but it is very much like saying that a spade is a spade is a spade. Whatever it is, it is the fundamental, basic, essential, primary cause of practically every action we take. Everywhere there is danger—but danger that we disregard. Statistics will demonstrate that you may cross the road a million and one times, but that on the million and second occasion you will fall under a bus or car. So the mere possibility of such and such a disaster being likely to occur does not in the least deter us from crossing the road. The presence of courage, and the feeling we all know that characterizes it, is complemented by its polar opposite, namely, *fear.*

Fear is the primary, the overwhelmingly powerful feeling that characterizes the animal world. Animals live by fear, and thus instinctively avoid danger and preserve their existence. Just observe birds, and how nervous they are, and the countless species of wild creature that will perhaps look at you from a safe distance, and then at your slightest movement take flight. If animals are observed to act in any way 'courageously', you may be sure that you are imputing human qualities to them. Courage as such is a uniquely human trait, for it presupposes a sense of *self,* and only

human beings possess this. Inevitably involved with courage is *initiative*, and again this is found, in its 'pure' form,
only in people and not animals. Animals, for the most part,
simply succumb to their fear, and attempt to escape from the
source of danger or potential danger. We have to overcome
our fears and trepidations in a *conscious* way, and we need
courage to achieve this.

In all this it is clear that much of what we call 'instinct' in
terms of animal behaviour is for the most part the wisdom
innate in the group-ego of the various species which initiates
and regulates whatever activities are carried out and when
(for example, seasonal mating, eating habits, nest-building,
means of communication, and suchlike). The governing
drive of self-preservation is firmly rooted in the feeling of
fear, and this is clear evidence of the primal power of the
animals' *astral* nature. Where human beings are concerned
the individual ego is capable of controlling or subduing this
astral principle, although everyday life provides plenty of
examples where our emotional nature is allowed to take
precedence! The expression 'giving way to our feelings' is
indicative of this, but at the same time attempts to negate or
otherwise suppress our life of feeling lead to problems of
their own. Our feelings are also there to be enjoyed!

A small child seems fearless, and therefore needs careful
watching. This is largely because its consciousness of self
is almost entirely absent during its infant years. This is of
course because the incarnating spirit-filled ego has only
just begun its task of subjugating, so to speak, the three
vehicles available to it, namely, the astral, etheric and
physical 'bodies'. It is only when the first signs that the
ego is beginning to take firm hold that acts of genuine
courage are possible. This time is also marked by increased
wilfulness, the appearance of a rudimentary conceptual
memory to supplement its mainly pictorial memory, its
ability to look forward, to take a realistic attitude to the
passage of time, and other indications that the selfhood

factor is now at work. Certain measures can be taken early on in a child's life, but later it may not be so easy to work out just how much freedom a child should have in order to develop courage.

Initially, a baby has absolute trust in its parents and will be guided by its mother and father. But later on, as you will know, it wants to try things out without adult interference. However, it is the adult who knows that there are consequences to actions, and these are not known by a child and therefore not anticipated. This kind of *inconsequential behaviour* is what all parents and carers have to take account of, and this is touched on in Chapter 8. If possible, a child should be guided by firm action rather than over-fussiness. If a child is being constantly forbidden and denied it will become fidgety and unhappy, and good sleep may not result from this adult interference. Of course, any hazards to safety must be checked. Be suspicious of sudden quiet! It is not wise to leave a child in the bathroom alone, especially if the water is running for the bath, for example. Many activities can be turned to account by building up a child's courage, but generally speaking new experiences should be engaged in under close but discreet scrutiny. A nervous mother will affect the courage and initiative of her child, even if this is not put into words.

As we keep on saying, your child will first imitate you; then when it is older it will listen to what you say. After puberty he or she will try all sorts of things out, and you will just have to trust that family values are ingrained and that your child has enough courage—a strong enough ego—to stand up and be counted, against the opinion of the majority if required to do so. Fairy-stories and folk tales heard in childhood will spring to mind when 'danger' threatens, and the hero will be an example of being capable of continuing courage. The stories of courageous people in history who stood up for what they believed in will also build up courage in a child and adolescent. Probably all we can really maintain is that a well-integrated personality at adulthood will have the courage of his or her convictions because decisions may be made from as wide a range of options as possible. Such a person will be able to think for himself or herself despite what others think, and decisions made from clear logical thinking may not please others. Strong personalities in history who are remembered for what they did for others have had a considerable influence upon people's thinking to this day.

Have courage for the truth

So much is happening so quickly in the world at present, and so much is not disclosed to the majority of citizens that inevitably a distrust of authority—politicians and decision-makers behind the scenes—and the numbers of shifty financiers, lawyers, and others who manipulate trade deals at high levels are growing. We are now at the stage where we must have an awareness of how people react in different circumstances in life so that we are not over-whelmed within ourselves by the remarks of those in authority who may not 'think with their heart', but who make decisions based on their own vested interests. Scientists make 'discoveries', and others long to be part of the 'team' in the limelight. A new technique in surgery is developed—and as a result surgeons need someone to practise on. It used to be the fashion to remove tonsils, adenoids or appendixes. However, now it is cosmetic surgery, external and internal, that is popular, as is the acquisition of someone's organs to sew into someone else. However, it also takes a certain courage to refuse to respond to government encouragement to 'donate' our organs in case of fatal accident or other terminal circumstance. Animal hearts and other parts are not now so popular; they didn't 'take' to start with, but rest assured that the problem is being worked on—this time in the direction of including human genes in relatively compatible animals such as the pig. Our children need parents with courage so that they in turn may have the boldness to question and think about where we are heading in our aberrant civilization.

Wading through the information available these days is difficult. For at least two decades people have been commenting on the tremendous and rapid upsurge in information technology, and the various facts and figures are available in forms that were not dreamed of before the advent of the twentieth century. We cannot keep track of it all but we need to know what is going on in the world, so how do we maintain our courage in order to cope with the stresses and strains of these times? Rudolf Steiner was firm in his assertions that children should not be taught in such a way that they acquired rigid concepts. Just as a pair of shoes that would fit a child of, say, eight years would not fit it in subsequent years, and certainly not in adulthood, so should 'characteristics' be given to a child during its schooling in such a way that these can be absorbed and this 'knowledge' grow with the child.[1] This knowledge can then be used as a basis for more informed judgements and decisions.

Classical literature contains truths

Much more about this is given in the chapter on education. However, to recapitulate on several examples, we mention the fairy-tales with their ancient wisdom; the folk tales with their treatment of human behaviour and trickery; those who fought with great courage for a cause they were prepared to die for; and the story of a human journey in the Old Testament and the indications for the future in the New Testament. Throughout all of these, the knowledge of higher worlds is hinted at, and revealed in story form. Now, however, we gain courage to strengthen our ego through knowledge of key events in the past, wakefulness to events in our own time, and to an appreciation of where we are heading. The common thread is that of gaining knowledge of the human being and, in so doing, learning to know our own self and its nature.

The emphasis on knowledge as being the acquisition of as many facts as possible and keeping up with the latest trends in the various areas of life is misleading. Putting all one's faith in scientific knowledge and technology rather than learning to think for ourselves keeps us 'scattered' rather than 'centred' in our inner world, and so must be suspect. To progress we must have an inner quiet in order to hear what is not said but rather intuited. We must have courage to recognize the good in the world and to fight against what is evil, although wickedness may be regarded by some people as merely a concept with no intrinsic reality. Many of the pleasures we can comparatively easily indulge in and enjoy are the most distracting as well as being detrimental to our own welfare in this incarnation, and perhaps in subsequent incarnations also.

Human relationships are not easy

Probably more fortitude is needed in these times than in any time in our past. Courage is needed in order to face everyday interaction with other people. The most common kind of crisis to be faced again and again in different ways, and in ways not yet envisaged, is that which concerns social relationships. Now, as never before, people are estranged from one another and they feel isolated and alone. Loneliness is a condition that is becoming a universal problem for those who are more ego-conscious—and people *are* becoming more ego-conscious, and often more egotistic with it. Individuals long to be loved, and long to be the most important person in someone else's life—and generally a permanent relationship is desired. However, this is more difficult to realize than ever before in history.

We have explained elsewhere that as a result of the

excessively intellectual and therefore one-sided education system in most western countries, people are becoming less warm-hearted towards one another. The widespread tendency to adopt an analytic, scientifically objective approach leaves the feelings untouched, and indeed 'hardens the heart' physically and emotionally. Relationships on all levels of life are now affected, generally for the worse. The education systems, based on intense competition and accountability through exam results, are crushing the souls of both children and adults. In this regard this warning that Steiner issued in 1919 in *Education as a Social Problem* is as relevant today as it was then:

> ... if we are to bring about a true form of society it must be prepared through people's education. To this end we must not proceed in a small way but on a large scale; for our (state) education system has gradually taken on a character that leads directly to what I described yesterday as mechanization of the spirit, vegetation of the soul, and animalization of the body. We must not follow this direction ...[2]

Those children with supportive parents and good memories succeed better than those who are not so well endowed for the acquisition of knowledge, when in fact they may have more skills and qualities than the others, intangible qualities which are not measured, and which are certainly not treasured in this day and age. School reports generally do not include descriptors such as 'has initiative, shows honesty, is caring, is thoughtful, thorough, careful, punctual and reliable'. Now everything must be included in categories which can be measured and evaluated. What happens within, what effects our education system has on children's inner life will never be known, but attempted and accomplished suicides are increasing, particularly among young men.

Our collapsing society

Family relationships are under unimagined stresses because of amazingly rapid and disconcerting changes in circumstances at home and at work. The 'growth industry' is that concerned with human relationships, whether it is to do with 'supporting' children, victims of crime, mentally unstable people, parents and relatives of missing persons, prisoners, the unemployed or whoever—which are collapsing in all areas of people's lives. Euthanasia is a matter of popular concern nowadays, as is suicide and homicide. Obviously, every creature that is born, or becomes imbued with life, must die—the one is the consequence of the other. But as we have implied throughout, the process is not just a single ticket. Return tickets there are, because death must imply another life. And so the round trips go on, but in ever-heightening spirals.

Of course, we must all face death, but when pressed people generally say that they are not so much afraid of dying; rather it is the *idea* of it that scares them, and not knowing just *how* it is going to occur. It is this idea that as the years and decades go by people have to 'fight', for it is there as an ever-present reality which is construed as a *threat*. None of us likes to be threatened, for this so often gives rise to fear, and then fear becomes the threat ... So it goes on, and it all becomes confusing and worrying. We do not subscribe to the view that life must be 'beer and skittles' or 'eat, drink and be merry, for tomorrow we die', because our individual task in life has, we believe, been chosen in order to work for the good of others—even though this involves pain and suffering and continuing hard work in whatever circumstance we find ourselves. If it isn't accomplished this time, it will need more work —albeit of a different kind—in our next incarnation on earth, when we too will be reincarnating children dependent on our 'parents'.

The problem of pain and illness

Some people stay healthy all their lives, and die in their sleep; these we all envy. Most of us undergo pain and suffering of some kind, often in the form of chronic illness or disability, congenital or acquired. Of course, coughs and colds, aches and sprains, slight injuries and so on are not being referred to in this section. It is the serious, significant maladies or disabilities, which are sufficiently grave as to hamper expectations of the average healthy person, that involve us here. In his book *Blessed by Illness*, Dr L. F. C. Mees makes out a convincing case for this ideal.[3] We, by our very predisposition to certain illnesses, have as it were provided for them to occur by reason of the operation of the law of karma or self-created destiny. We will have brought serious accidents, diseases and disabilities about by our own unconscious volition, and for a specific purpose, which however will accord to the general overall intention and objective of *progressing along the path towards perfection.*[4]

This may seem of academic interest only to those who are fit and well, and stay that way. But where deaf, blind, and severely physically or psychologically disabled people are concerned, including those suffering from life-threatening ailments such as cancer, chronic heart disease, epilepsy, diabetes and so on, interest in the latest forms of treatment is keen. They are the last people who need Job's comforters around them, for, as Rudyard Kipling neatly put it:

> The toad beneath the harrow knows
> Exactly where each tooth-point goes.
> The butterfly upon the road
> Preaches contentment to that toad.

Of course it is difficult for anyone at first to come to the realization that they are ultimately responsible for their own condition, whether in sickness or in health, fully to accept it and live with it. But this is where *courage* comes in—we need plenty of it! People who stay disgustingly fit are usually those who fear illness and disability most, because they do not know whether thay will be able to 'take it' if—but usually when—their time for trial arrives, which it almost certainly will sooner or later.

A general attitude of stoicism is obviously called for, together with certain elements of patience and long-suffering, and perhaps an even-mindedness bordering on sheer resignation. Very often a person's life-style is dramatically affected for the worse, and this calls for enormous reserves of courage, determination and sheer grit. That's the bad news. The good news is that people invariably—we almost said always—rise to the occasion in truly magnificent fashion, wholly conquering their fears and apprehensions, their pain and discomfort, their disappointments and disabilities arising. It says a very great deal for the enormous capacity of resilience and adaptability of people to pain and suffering; it is truly astounding, as we have experienced personally. Furthermore, people who undergo such experience invariably—again we almost said always—emerge as better people in every possible way. They for the most part become as contented as they can possibly be with their new life-style and circumstances, though it will usually have cost them dear in terms of emotional and mental anguish. But most will admit to their becoming 'better people' as a result of their sufferings. And a kind of 'added benefit' is obtained by others, ordinary healthy people—friends and acquaintances mostly—who are inspired, encouraged and heartened by the 'victims of circumstance' who 'paid the price' in terms of pain, distress and misery.

'Riddle of destiny ... '

> Riddle of destiny, who can show
> What thy short visit meant, or know
> What thy errand here below?

This question, put by the essayist Charles Lamb in his poem *On an Infant Dying as soon as Born*, surely finds echoes in very many hearts of distraught and anguished parents. Here again, the answer must be looked for in the law of self-created destiny, and comfort sought in the necessary and complementary law of reincarnation. People usually regard these twin notions as matters of belief only, but there is so much support for them on philosophical, religious, historical, traditional and other grounds as to render them much more feasible than the 'one and only life, and then oblivion' notion. The same position obtains when children die young, perhaps of cancer, cystic fibrosis, muscular dystrophy or a score of other congenital disorders. Grief and distress are of course a perfectly normal reaction, but there is also comfort in the realization that spiritual laws will bring it about that they will meet again in the same or future life. The view that children who die young not infrequently make a very rapid return to earth, perhaps to the same family or a near relative, may well be a source of solace and comfort to many a grief-stricken family. It bears repetition in this regard that a 'child' is actually a *mature ego*, ageless and immortal, who will almost certainly have chosen to make a 'sacrifice' of some kind for reasons we cannot determine.

The number of suicides, especially among young people, increases steadily year by year. Suicide is mentioned in connection with the soul forces in the chapter on discipline. We do not test children and young people in regard to their individual qualities.[5] The world is now such an unpleasant, even nasty place in many respects that this is not surprising. Here again we have a problem involving courage, this time whether the fear of life is stronger than the fear of death, and this is a highly individual matter. The 'oblivion' school has little to say on the matter apart from stating that if the pain and suffering becomes unbearable there is nothing to lose by taking an overdose or jumping off the bridge. Doing away with oneself in this fashion, or by euthanasia, is regarded by many as the epitome of selfishness. Not only do suicides leave behind grieving friends and relations, but the problem which drove them to their death might well have been willingly alleviated by those very same people had they known of it. To the thinking of those who maintain the realities of reincarnation and self-created destiny, the same kind of problem will also remain, only to reappear in a later existence. There is no escape from the system, and even to common-sense thinking this is only fair and wise. For were it not so, civilization would not have progressed as it has and individuals would not have had the necessary opportunities to advance.

Our urge to know and understand

Whatever else may be said about fear as having a right and proper function in our daily lives, mainly as a kind of alerting or warning facility in potentially dangerous situations, it is nevertheless true that much of the fear and trepidation we experience is because of the *unknown*. Knowledge of what is going on is often an enormous help in 'defusing' situations in which fear plays a significant part. In this respect, ignorance is a very real handicap, and the maxim 'Knowledge is power' springs to mind. The more we know and realize about a given circumstance the less trepidation is likely to be involved. But this may be counter-balanced by the saying 'Ignorance is bliss when it's folly to be wise'! On balance, however, the overwhelming urge for us to *know and understand* what is going on around us defeats any 'head in the sand' attitude.

The great value of Rudolf Steiner's courage and tenacity, not to mention sheer ability, was the adding of a *genuine science of the spirit* to the already existing enormous body of knowledge amassed by empirical, material science. The results of his dedicated work in the area of investigation and research into the spiritual worlds has done much in enabling us to know and understand much of what goes on in the world of matter. This very knowledge is itself a factor in explaining much that has been hitherto inexplicable, and is of tremendous value in, as it were, putting our minds at rest over certain critical problems and concerns we encounter every day in our private and social lives. These include insights into the nature and purpose of pain and suffering, disease and death, fortune and destiny, and other riddles of existence. Knowledge concerning issues such as these frequently result in lowering the power of the *fear factor* in human life and affairs, with the result that tendencies towards worry and stress give way to positive attitudes such as serenity of soul and contentment of spirit. Above all, perhaps, a genuine, concrete knowledge and understanding of ourselves as human beings is the most powerful stabilizing factor of all—and this is what Dr Steiner gave us. He continually emphasized the importance of everyone being able to develop his or her own talents in order to develop clarity of thought, deepening of feeling, and the greatest possible energy and ability of will, in order to find their place in life. To quote him:

> The great essential is for men and women to be wide-hearted, to be able to participate with their hearts and souls in culture and civilization as a whole ... That, my dear friends, is the attitude underlying the art of education of which I have been speaking to you. It is based wholly on this principle: the measures adopted in education and teaching must be derived from the very being of man, so that on the one hand human beings shall develop to full adulthood in body, soul, and spirit, and on the other that they shall find their place in life, having in childhood—again in body, soul, and spirit— grown up in a religious, ethical, artistic and intellectual life and so have been enabled to develop virtues best fitted to be of use to their fellow human beings.[6]

Hope and despair

Earlier on we mentioned the present dolorous state of the world. Well, you will say, people were responsible for this, so why do they themselves create such a wicked and unpleasant environment, destroying so much that is beautiful, good and true? The answer must be that we—collectively—have deliberately created those dreadful social conditions, polluted land, sea and air, and brought on all the rest of our troubles. Some of these have their roots in ignorance of the consequences, but that does not alter the *fact* in any way; we are landed with it, and must choose, deliberately and with forethought, and to the best of our ability turn around and improve matters. So of course, eventually this is what we, or our descendants, will do, because we are, after all, beings of intelligence and resourcefulness—aren't we?

Very often our only grounds for hope consist in our knowledge of the circumstances and situation, and our understanding of these. Despair is very often born of the very lack of ability to come to grips with dire circumstances. If the outlook is grim, then we need the courage—and perhaps optimism—to face such predicaments, and this kind of attitude is far preferable to one of panic-stricken despair. As Sir James Barrie averred: 'Courage is the thing. All goes if courage goes.' 'True grit' is a characteristic of individuals whose ego is sufficiently strong to, as it were, hold himself or herself together, and this presupposes a well-integrated ego—which is what this book is all about.

The extent to which we possess courage is the measure of our progress along our individual path to perfection, which we are all treading whether we realize it or not. Eventually, realization must come, and for this we must all know and understand the nature of the immaterial world as well as the material, and in this we owe the greatest possible debt to Rudolf Steiner, whose matchless courage in face of every adversity serves as an example to all pilgrims.

We must eradicate from the soul all fear and terror of what comes towards mankind out of the future. We must look forward with absolute equanimity to all that may come and we must think only that whatever comes is given to us by a world direction full of wisdom. It is part of what we must learn in this age, namely, to live out of pure trust, without any security in existence: trust in the ever-present help of the spiritual world. Truly, nothing else will do if our courage is not to fail us. Let us discipline our will, and let us seek the awakening from within ourselves, every morning and every evening.[7]

Rudolf Steiner

Notes and References

Chapter 1

1. Steiner, R., *Occult Science—an Outline*, Anthroposophic Press 1939, *passim*.
2. Childs, G. J., *Steiner Education in Theory and Practice*, Floris Books 1991, *passim*.
   Note: We have not dealt in great depth in this book with this important and complex subject because it is fully set out in *Education and Beyond*, (forthcoming) Floris Books 1996, and in a forthcoming companion volume to this book by Gilbert Childs.
3. Steiner, R., *The Kingdom of Childhood*, Rudolf Steiner Press 1964, p. 25.
4. Childs, G. J., *Steiner Education in Theory and Practice*, Chapter 5.
5. Steiner, R., 'Education in the Science of Spirit' in *Education as an Art*, Rudolf Steiner Publishing Co. 1970, p. 26.

Chapter 2

1. MacDonald, G., *At the Back of the North Wind*, J. M. Dent, n.d., p. 278.
2. Glas, N., *Conception, Birth, and Early Childhood*, Anthroposophic Press 1983, *passim*.
3. *Ibid.*, p. 14.
4. *Ibid.*, p. 17.
5. *Ibid.*, p. 15.
6. Bott, V., *Anthroposophical Medicine*, Rudolf Steiner Press 1982, p. 84.
7. Glas, N., *op. cit.*, p. 19.
   Note: (a) The incarnating ego, in co-operation with the spiritual hierarchies, strives to arrange its appearance on earth for the time and circumstances most propitious to its interests. The influences of the planets of our solar system and the 'fixed' stars have a very real

influence in all this. For example, during gestation the embryo and foetus experience the sun's transit through approximately nine zodiacal signs or parts thereof. The main influences of the two or three signs that were thereby 'missed' are to be experienced during the individual's subsequent earthly sojourn.

(b) The axis of the earth is inclined at an angle of 21.5 degrees—the precise angle at which the human heart is set in the chest.

(c) The breathing rate of a human adult at rest averages 18 per minute. This means that during 24 hours 18 x 60 x 24 = 25,920 breaths are taken—the precise number of years (equals one so-called 'Platonic Year') that it takes for the sun, by reason of the phenomenon known to astronomers as the precession of the vernal equinoxes, to complete a 'path' around the earth.

8   *Ibid.*, pp. 32–33.
9   *Ibid.*, pp. 45–47.
10   Steiner, R., *The Renewal of Education*, Kolisko Archive Publications, for Steiner Schools Fellowship Publications, p. 48.

Chapter 3
1   Glas, N., *op cit.*, p. 37.
2   zur Linden, W., quoted in Glas, N., *op cit.*, p. 38.
3   Brackbill, Y., 'Cumulative Effects of Continuous Stimulation on Arousal Levels in Infants', *Child Development* 1971, p. 42.
4   Glas, N., *op. cit.*, p. 46.
5   Steiner, R., *Human Values in Education*, Rudolf Steiner Press 1971, p. 44.
6   Schubert, I., *Reminiscences of Rudolf Steiner*, Temple Lodge 1991, p. 90.
7   Glas, N., *op. cit.*, p. 44.
8   Pringle, K. M., *The Needs of Children*, Century

Hutchinson, 3rd edition 1986, p. 34.

9   Steiner, R., *Metamorphoses of the Soul*, Rudolf Steiner Publishing Co., n.d., p. 119.

Chapter 4

1   Steiner, R., *Study of Man*, Rudolf Steiner Publishing Co. 1979, pp. 99–102.
2   Forthcoming companion volume to this book, by Gilbert Childs.
3   Note: Weleda is a worldwide organization that provides a wide range of pharmaceutical products, available at many chemists, that have been developed from indications given by Rudolf Steiner.
4   Godwin, M., *Angels: an Endangered Species*, Boxtree 1993.
     Davidson, G., *A Dictionary of Angels*, The Free Press 1971.
5   Steiner, R., *Study of Man*, pp. 21–22.
6   Forthcoming companion volume to this book, by Gilbert Childs, Chapter 5.
7   Steiner, R., *Study of Man*, lecture 9, p. 138.
8   Bott, V., *op. cit.*, p. 88.
9   Steiner, R., *A Modern Art of Education*, Rudolf Steiner Press, 3rd edition, 1981, p. 115.
10   *Ibid.*, p. 112.
11   Steiner, R., *Study of Man*, pp 9–10.

Chapter 5

1   Bott, V., *op. cit.*, p. 28.
2   Note: Although not dealing specifically with this question, the following book is recommended for an in-depth understanding of colour from spiritual-scientific and aesthetic points of view: Schindler, M., *Pure Colour*, Rudolf Steiner Press 1989.

3   Read, H., *The Meaning of Art*, Pelican 1947, p. 196.

Chapter 6
1   Knauer, I., *The Feeding of Children*, New Knowledge Books, n.d., p. 12.
2   Hauschka, R., *Nutrition*, Rudolf Steiner Press 1983, p. 189.
3   *Ibid.*, p. 190.
4   *Ibid.*, p. 14.
5   Glas, N., *op. cit.*, pp. 50–51.
6   Bott, V., *op. cit.*, p. 87.
7   Hauschka, R., *op. cit.*, p. 192.

Chapter 7
1   Childs, G. J., *Steiner Education in Theory and Practice*, p. 103.
2   Steiner, R., *The Roots of Education*, Rudolf Steiner Press 1968, p. 44.
3   Steiner, R., *Education and Modern Spiritual Life*, Anthroposophical Publishing Co., 3rd edition 1954, pp. 115–119.
4   Steiner, R., *The Child's Changing Consciousness and Waldorf Education*, Anthroposophic Press 1988, lecture VIII, *passim*.
5   Note: See Reading List, p. 178.
6   Childs, G. J., *Steiner Education in Theory and Practice*, pp. 118–119.
7   Glas, N., *op. cit.*, p. 97.
8   *Ibid.*
9   *Op. cit.*, p. 98.
10   McAllen, A. E., notes taken at lecture and oral communication to S. C.
11   McAllen, A. E., *Teaching Children to Write*, A. E. McAllen 1977, pp. 15–16.

12 Baldwin, R., *You Are Your Child's First Teacher*, Celestial Arts 1989, p. 220.
13 Steiner, R., *The Child's Changing Consciousness and Waldorf Education*, Anthroposophic Press 1988, pp. 79–81.

Chapter 8
1 Gabert, E., *Educating the Adolescent: Discipline or Freedom?*, Rudolf Steiner Press 1968, p. 15.
2 Steiner, R., *The Kingdom of Childhood*, pp. 20–21.
3 Pringle, K. M., *op. cit.*, p. 103.
4 Childs, G. J., *Steiner Education in Theory and Practice*, p. 63.
5 Steiner, R., *The Inner Realities of Evolution*, pp. 58–59.
6 *Ibid.*
7 Gabert, E., *op. cit.*, p. 9.
8 *Ibid.*
9 Childs, G. J., *Steiner Education in Theory and Practice*, Chapter 10 and *passim*.
10 Woolfson, R. C., *Understanding Your Child; a Parent's Guide to Child Psychology*, Faber and Faber 1989, p. 138.
11 Gabert, E., *op. cit.*, pp. 15–16.

Chapter 9
1 Mander, J., *Four Arguments for the Elimination of Television*, Harvester Press 1980, p. 348.
2 *Op. cit.*, pp. 189–90.
3 *Op. cit.*, p. 133.
4 *Op. cit.*, pp. 167–168.
5 Note: *The Times* newspaper article (December 1993) reviewed a study, conducted by Minnesota's Concordia College students, on violence in television programmes in the USA. Television viewers in the USA can see more than one thousand acts of violence a week, according to that study. Violence was defined as 'the deliberate use

of force by one individual against another', and included murders, stabbings, fights, chases, explosions, shooting, suicide, property damage, poisoning, drugging and threats of violence. The senator who requested that the study be undertaken said: 'Children imitate what they see on television, that's the problem.' Violence on television in the United States has apparently escalated in recent years, and Congress has been concerned about this as one of the causes of crime and violence among children and teenagers.

6   Mander, J., *op. cit.*, pp. 15–16.
7   Peper, E., quoted in Mander, *op. cit.*, p. 211.
8   Woolfson, R. C., *op. cit.*, p. 48.
9   *Ibid.*, p. 52.
10 Note: not 'modelling' at all ages as used by psychologists.
11 Woolfson, R. C., *op.cit.*, p. 52.
12 Note: See also Winn, M., *The Plug-in Drug*, Bantam Books 1978; and Large, M., *Who's Bringing Them Up?*, Hawthorn Press, n.d.
13 Sandberg-Diment, E., *Computers and General Education* (quoted in *Child and Man*, January 1988, Vol. 22, No. 1).
14 Winn, M., *Children Without Childhood*, Penguin 1983, p. 79.
15 Steiner, R., *Education as a Social Problem*, Anthroposophic Press 1969, pp. 84–85.
16 Winn, M., *The Plug-in Drug*, Bantam Books 1978, p. 247.

Chapter 10
1   Note: For further discussion and elucidation please refer to Childs, G. J., S*teiner Education in Theory and Practice*, Chapters 5 and 14.
2   Steiner, R., *Education as a Social Problem*, Anthroposophic Press 1969, p. 45.
3   Mees, L. F. C., *Blessed by Illness*, Anthroposophic Press 1983, *passim*.

4   Childs, G. J., *The Realities of Prayer*, Sophia Books 1994, Chapter 6.
5   Steiner, R., *Education as a Social Problem*, p. 78.
6   Steiner, R., *A Modern Art of Education*, p. 211.
7   Steiner, R., source unable to be traced. Circularized typescript which gave wrong date and location as checked against *Das Vortragswerk Rudolf Steiners*, Philosophisch-Anthroposophischer Verlag 1950.

Suggestions for Further Reading

Forthcoming companion volume to this book, by Gilbert Childs

From Rudolf Steiner Press (by R. Steiner, except where otherwise stated):
Reincarnation and Karma
The Inner Nature of Man
Christianity as Mystical Fact
Learning to See into the Spiritual World
The Course of My Life (Autobiography)
The Bible and Wisdom
Towards Social Renewal
The Fulfilment of Old Age, Norbert Glas

From Hawthorn Press:
Festivals, Family and Food, D. Carey and J. Large
The Children's Year, S. Cooper *et. al.*
The Incarnating Child, J. Salter
Lifeways, G. Davy and B. Voors
Fal the Dragon Harper, Peter Patterson (for older children)

From Floris Books:
A Guide to Child Health, Michaela Glöckler and Wolfgang Goebel
The Wisdom of Fairy Tales, Rudolf Meyer
The Christmas Craft Book, Thomas Berger
The Easter Craft Book, Thomas and Petra Berger
The Nature Corner, M. van Leeuwen and J. Moeskops
The Harvest Craft Book, Thomas Berger
Felt Craft, Petra Berger
Making Dolls, Sunnhild Reinnckens
Toy-making with Children, Freya Jaffke

Painting with Children, Brunhild Müller
Earth, Water, Fire and Air, Walter Kraul
* Plus an extensive list of children's story books

From Temple Lodge Publishing:
Snow White and the Seven Dwarfs
The Green Snake and the Beautiful Lily, dramatized by Benedict Wood
Parzival, Eileen Hutchins
The Mystery of Growing Up, Evelyn Francis Capel
Understanding Death, Evelyn Francis Capel

From Wynstones Press
Birthday, Norah Romer
Mother Earth's Children, Heather Jarman
with others suitable for young children